THE TRILLIONAIRE CLUB

THE TRILLIONAIRE CLUB

THE MORAL MANDATE TO END GLOBAL HUNGER

JD ROSSETTI

Copyright © 2025 by Juxtapolitico

Juxtapolitico.com

All rights reserved.

No part of this book may be reproduced in any form or by any electronic or mechanical means, including information storage and retrieval systems, without written permission from the author, except for the use of brief quotations in a book review.

For Humanity

More than 3 million children die from hunger-related causes every year. That's over 8,000 per day. Roughly one child every ten seconds.

In 2024, there wasn't a single trillionaire.

This book is not about blaming the rich for the completely preventable deaths.

It's about giving trillionaires a mandate.

It's about giving humanity a guarantee.

FOREWORD

The Trillionaire Club
A blueprint for moral wealth and global survival
The Wealth, the Power, and the Moral Mandate to End Global Hunger

What if the richest people on Earth weren't just powerful—they were responsible for feeding the world?

In *The Trillionaire Club*, JD Rossetti delivers a provocative, solution-driven exploration of how unimaginable wealth could be transformed into the force that finally ends world hunger and ensures universal access to clean water. As we stand on the cusp of the first trillion-dollar personal fortunes, Rossetti asks the question the world can no longer afford to ignore:

What is the moral obligation of the ultra-wealthy in a world where children still starve and millions drink unsafe water?

This isn't another book about inequality—it's a plan. *The Trillionaire Club* proposes a groundbreaking global policy: once someone reaches a trillion-dollar net worth, they are automatically enrolled in a binding international committee tasked with eradicating hunger and water insecurity. If the committee fails, its members are taxed proportionally to fulfill the need—no excuses, no opt-outs.

Drawing from international law, moral philosophy, economic modeling, and real-world success stories, Rossetti lays out a framework for how this bold vision could become reality—with transparency, enforceability, and unstoppable global momentum.

A gripping mix of exposé, manifesto, and blueprint, *The Trillionaire Club* is a must-read for activists, policymakers, economists, and everyday citizens who believe that wealth should serve a purpose greater than personal legacy.

Because when you have everything, you owe the world something.

PREFACE

Subject: Proposal for a UN Resolution to Eliminate Global Hunger and Ensure Universal Access to Clean Water through Global Trillionaire Responsibility

Dear United Nations Ambassador,

I hope this message finds you well. I am writing to respectfully submit a proposed resolution for your consideration and possible sponsorship within the United Nations General Assembly. This proposal, titled **"Toward the Elimination of Global Hunger and Universal Access to Clean Water through Proportional Responsibility of Ultra-High-Net-Worth Individuals,"** offers a bold yet realistic framework to address two of the most fundamental rights enshrined in international law—access to food and clean water.

At its core, the resolution suggests that individuals whose personal net worth exceeds one trillion US dollars should be automatically enrolled in a **Global Committee for Food and Water Security,** with a proportional responsibility to fund and support the global eradication of hunger and water scarcity. If unmet hunger or water needs remain, a financial responsibility clause would ensure coverage through equitable contribution.

The moral premise is simple: *those with the greatest wealth must carry a tangible responsibility for the most essential human needs.* The policy is structured, enforceable, and aligned with existing Sustainable Development Goals (SDG 2 and SDG 6). It complements current UN efforts with an innovative accountability mechanism for the modern global economy.

I have included the full draft of the proposed resolution along with a public-facing charter that has begun to circulate through policy, philanthropic, and academic communities. I would be honored to discuss the resolution with your office and explore the possibility of your nation championing this vital initiative at the United Nations.

Thank you for your time, your service, and your continued leadership on the world stage.

Warm regards,

JD Rossetti

THE GLOBAL TRILLIONAIRE RESPONSIBILITY CHARTER

The Global Trillionaire Responsibility Charter
A Declaration for the Elimination of Hunger and the Universal Right to Clean Water
By JD Rossetti

PREAMBLE

We, the citizens of Earth—united not by nation, creed, or fortune, but by shared humanity—declare that no one should die of hunger while another holds the wealth of nations.

In an age where one individual can possess more than the GDP of entire countries, it is no longer acceptable to treat extreme wealth as a personal triumph divorced from public consequence. The world now demands a new covenant: that those with the power to end suffering bear the responsibility to do so.

. . .

ARTICLE I – The Moral Obligation of Wealth

All individuals whose net worth reaches or exceeds **one trillion US dollars** shall bear a universal moral obligation to uphold the fundamental human rights to **nutritious food** and **clean, safe water** for all members of the global population.

This responsibility is not voluntary, symbolic, or charitable. It is structural, ongoing, and enforceable.

ARTICLE II – Formation of the Universal Committee for Human Sustenance

A **Universal Committee for Human Sustenance** shall be formed, composed of all trillionaires, to:

- Assess annual global hunger and clean water needs;
- Allocate strategic financial contributions and technological expertise;
- Implement sustainable, efficient delivery systems in collaboration with existing NGOs, public agencies, and private enterprise.

Committee membership is **automatic** upon reaching the trillionaire threshold and shall remain active as long as the threshold is met.

ARTICLE III – Accountability Through Consequence

If global hunger and clean water benchmarks are not met by the committee, each member shall be subject to a **proportional financial responsibility tax**, assessed annually. This tax shall be scaled to cover the unmet needs for the projected population in the following year.

This ensures that inaction or failure results not in blame —but in binding restitution.

ARTICLE IV – **Transparency and Public Oversight**
The actions of the Committee shall be **publicly visible** and tracked through an open-access dashboard, allowing all citizens of the world to monitor:
- Funding contributions
- Project deployment and outcomes
- Progress toward hunger and water elimination goals

Audits shall be conducted annually by a neutral body under international oversight.

ARTICLE V – **The Right to Basic Survival**
We affirm, without exception, that **access to nutritious food and clean water is a human right**—not a luxury, not a market commodity, and not a charitable gift.

No policy, profit, or patent shall supersede the sacred right of every person to live without starvation or preventable disease caused by waterborne contaminants.

CALL TO ACTION
We call upon:
- **Governments** to ratify this framework into law and tax policy;
- **Global organizations** to adopt this model into sustainable development goals;
- **Citizens** to demand responsibility from the ultra-wealthy;
- And **trillionaires** to step forward not as symbols of excess, but as stewards of human survival.

The world has enough wealth. It needs enough will.

The time to align prosperity with purpose is now.

SIGNED IN GLOBAL SOLIDARITY,
JD Rossetti
Author, Citizen, Advocate for a Just Future

1

THE TRILLIONAIRE ERA
THE NEW ARISTOCRACY

In the early years of the 21st century, the term "trillionaire" belonged more to the lexicon of science fiction than economics. It conjured images of futuristic tycoons owning space stations or terraforming planets —not real people with real influence over the fate of billions. But today, that fiction is fast becoming fact.

As we edge closer to the rise of the world's first trillionaire—likely in the next decade—we find ourselves confronting a reality we've never known: a single human being with more financial power than most governments, institutions, and global humanitarian organizations combined.

This chapter begins with a simple observation: **we've entered a new aristocracy**, one not inherited through bloodlines but forged through capital gains, technological monopolies, and financial acceleration on a scale history has never seen. And unlike the feudal lords of past centuries, this new aristocracy is largely unbound by geography, regulation, or democratic accountability.

Let's be clear—wealth in and of itself is not a sin.

Progress, innovation, and industry have always created wealth, and rightly so. The problem is not that some have more than others. The problem is when a few have **so much more** than **everyone else** that they could literally solve civilization's most devastating crises—**but are not required to.**

The question at the heart of this book is simple:

Should anyone have the power to end hunger and not be obligated to try?

Trillionaires: The Next Class of Global Power

The idea of someone possessing one trillion dollars in personal net worth once seemed impossible. Today, financial projections show it's not only plausible—it's inevitable. Tech giants like Elon Musk, Jeff Bezos, and Bernard Arnault have flirted with the $200–300 billion range in recent years. If wealth continues to compound at current rates—driven by global markets, monopolistic business models, and algorithmic scaling—one or more of these individuals (or their successors) could cross the trillion-dollar threshold in a matter of years.

What does that mean in practical terms?

- A trillionaire could single-handedly fund universal food access for five years.
- A trillionaire could underwrite clean water infrastructure for half the planet.
- A trillionaire could eradicate malaria, cholera, and other waterborne illnesses in regions where entire nations lack sufficient budgets.

And yet, **no existing legal structure compels them to do so.** No social contract requires that level of wealth to correspond with global responsibility. In fact, today's global financial system is built to **protect, insulate,** and **defer**responsibility, not enforce it.

The New Invisible Power

In previous centuries, the ruling class was visible. Monarchs wore crowns. Aristocrats sat in palaces. Power was tied to land and lineage, and everyone knew who ruled. But today's wealth elite—especially those in the digital economy—exist largely behind screens, in private jets, encrypted holdings, and untouchable tax structures.

Their power is invisible, their influence omnipresent.

A single decision made by a trillionaire—such as buying out a company, funding a political lobbying campaign, or moving assets offshore—can send ripple effects across the global economy. Stock markets react. Nations adjust. Yet most of this occurs outside public oversight.

Where monarchs were bound by the fear of revolt or loss of divine favor, modern economic monarchs are bound by **nothing but their own discretion.** In most jurisdictions, there is no law, regulation, or even moral expectation demanding they address global humanitarian needs.

This is not because the world lacks mechanisms—it's because it has lacked the will to create them.

A New Kind of Social Contract

But here's the opportunity: just as we created global agreements for war crimes, environmental standards, and climate responsibility, we can create a **global economic covenant** for hunger and water security. One that recognizes not just the danger of extreme poverty—but the **danger of extreme wealth left ungoverned.**

Imagine if reaching one trillion dollars in net worth came with an automatic global mandate:

- You serve on a world committee for food and water security.
- You fund initiatives based on global need, proportional to your wealth.
- If unmet needs remain, you contribute further until they're resolved.

It's not punitive. It's proportional. And it's overdue.

As this book will argue, **we don't need to tax ambition. We need to tax indifference.** The age of the trillionaire should not be defined by luxury—it should be defined by leadership.

We are not proposing the abolition of wealth. We are proposing the **moral anchoring of it.**

Because in a world where one man can buy a rocket fleet while a million children die from malnutrition, **wealth becomes more than privilege—it becomes a test of character.**

This is the age we've entered. And it's only the beginning.

From Millionaire to Trillionaire — A 40-Year Trajectory

The path to a trillion-dollar personal fortune didn't begin with a single company, a sudden innovation, or a lottery-like leap in luck. It began with **policy, technology,** and **compounding scale**—a steady build over decades made possible by the structure of modern capitalism itself.

To understand how we got here—and why trillionaires are not an anomaly, but a feature of our global system—we must trace the arc of wealth creation over the past 40 years.

2.1 The Acceleration of Capital

In 1982, the Forbes 400 list of the richest Americans was topped by oil and industrial magnates. The wealthiest man in the world at the time, Daniel Ludwig, was worth approximately $2 billion. Adjusted for inflation, that's around $6 billion today—hardly modest, but a far cry from the multi-hundred-billion-dollar fortunes we now see.

What changed?

- **The rise of technology and platform economics** created businesses with near-zero marginal costs and infinite scalability. Once you build a digital product, distribution is virtually free.
- **Global deregulation and tax havens** allowed capital to be protected, hidden, and reinvested at compounding rates far greater than wages or GDP growth.
- **Venture capital and algorithmic investing** meant that returns accelerated not based on labor or goods, but on predictive models and user data.

By the 2000s, we saw our first individuals break the $50–100 billion net worth mark. By the 2020s, several surged past $200 billion.

Projecting forward, **the world's first trillionaire is expected within a decade**, depending on market conditions. Analysts from financial firms like Morgan Stanley and Credit Suisse forecast that if tech monopolies continue to grow—even with modest gains—the math is inevitable.

It's not a question of *if*. It's *when*.

And it will likely happen before the world solves hunger, clean water, climate collapse, or systemic poverty.

2.2 Compound Wealth vs. Compound Need

While wealth compounds geometrically, so do the world's humanitarian crises—just in reverse.

- Hunger is rising due to inflation, war, and climate disruptions.
- Water access is shrinking due to overuse, pollution, and drought.
- Supply chains for food and medicine are under pressure from global volatility.

And yet, the financial capacity of a handful of individuals has grown faster than the GDP of entire continents. Consider this comparison:

- The annual cost to end world hunger is estimated between $40–50 billion.
- A trillionaire could spend **that amount for 20 consecutive years** and still remain a multi-billionaire with wealth that earns back faster than it is spent.

This isn't speculation—it's simple math. What makes it shocking is not the math itself, but the **lack of global structures to act upon it.**

We have normalized the idea that wealth accumulates privately while crises remain public burdens. But that's a structural flaw, not a moral failing of one individual. The system enables and protects hoarding—because there is **no mandate to do otherwise.**

2.3 The Fragility of Billionaire Systems

One might argue that these high-net-worth individuals are "job creators," "innovators," or "economic engines"— and to an extent, that's true. Many have built products, platforms, and services that changed the world.

But that is not the issue.

The issue is that **wealth this extreme becomes systemically dangerous** when it:

- Concentrates influence beyond democratic reach,
- Avoids taxation while public services erode,
- And evades responsibility in a world drowning in solvable problems.

In the same way monopolies distort markets, **unregulated trillionaires distort humanity's priorities.**

Should one person's net worth be allowed to outweigh the budgets of 50 of the world's poorest countries combined?

Should humanitarian crises go unfunded while private space companies chart courses to Mars?

Should it be legal—not just possible—for wealth to accelerate while hunger increases?

These questions are not rhetorical. They are structural. They are solvable.

2.4 The Window Is Closing

As wealth trajectories rise, so too does public awareness of inequality. Movements like Occupy Wall Street, Extinction Rebellion, and the push for Universal Basic Income are symptoms of a deeper recognition:

The economic game has no referee.

There are rules, yes—but they are made by those who benefit most from the lack of enforcement.

The trillionaire era offers us a rare chance to rebalance that equation before it calcifies into permanent apartheid—one where a handful live above the clouds and the rest of us struggle to access food, water, or shelter.

This is not a call for revolution. It is a call for **responsible reinvention.**

We can acknowledge innovation, brilliance, and economic success—while also **building the mandate for global stewardship.** We can say, "Well done," and also say, "Now it's time to serve."

Because the line between wealth and wisdom is not crossed with another billion.

It's crossed with a choice.

The Invisibility of Power

Power used to wear a face. In monarchies, it sat on gilded thrones. In democracies, it took the form of elected office. In military regimes, it paraded in uniform. But in the modern financial era—particularly in the age of the soon-to-be trillionaire—**power has become invisible, unaccountable, and often untraceable.**

Trillionaire wealth isn't stashed in a vault. It doesn't sit in a single account or pile of cash. It's dispersed across stock portfolios, private equity, real estate, tax shelters, offshore trusts, algorithmically traded indexes, and opaque instruments that few people outside elite financial circles understand.

This is by design.

Extreme wealth has built itself **a fortress of abstraction—** layers of anonymity and legal complexity that allow those at the top to remain untouchable. The invisibility isn't just financial—it's ethical. The richer someone becomes, the less direct responsibility they seem to bear for the world around them.

This part explores how that invisibility was created, and why it must be dismantled—not to punish wealth, but to *anchor it to reality.*

3.1 The Shield of Complexity

It's no accident that trillionaire-class individuals often operate through shell companies, multijurisdictional tax havens, or decentralized asset networks. This ecosystem is built to avoid not only tax liability, but **moral liability**.

If assets are spread across 30 countries, who can hold them accountable? If foundations donate millions while shifting billions to family trusts, how can we evaluate impact?

The system enables plausible deniability. It obscures lines of cause and effect. The CEO of a trillion-dollar company can express "concern" about hunger in a PR statement while failing to fund even 0.1% of the solution, all while wealth compounds untouched.

This isn't a conspiracy. It's infrastructure. And the result is a **disconnection between power and responsibility** that no democracy or ethics-based society can survive indefinitely.

3.2 The Myth of the Self-Made Titan

Another powerful shield trillionaires hide behind is the myth of the "self-made" visionary. And yes, many of them are brilliant, hardworking, and even courageous in their ventures. But that does not absolve them from global obligations.

No one builds a trillion-dollar fortune alone. These fortunes exist because:

- Roads, schools, and digital infrastructure were publicly funded.
- Workers, customers, and consumers—across every country—fed into their ecosystems.
- Governments provided tax loopholes, legal protections, and sometimes bailouts.

To believe that such wealth is purely private creation is to erase the very public fabric that made it possible.

The myth of self-made success justifies disengagement. It says, "I earned it, so I owe nothing." But *The Trillionaire Club* challenges this idea and replaces it with a higher truth: **With great benefit comes binding responsibility.**

3.3 From Obscurity to Accountability

When no legal or institutional framework exists to require public contribution, even well-meaning wealth holders may default to silence. They are not pressured by law, shamed by public consensus, or nudged by systems to participate in solving the biggest problems of the human race.

It's time to change that.

To do so, we must:

- **Make wealth visible.**
- Require public net worth disclosures above a threshold, akin to campaign finance law or conflict-of-interest rules for public officials.
- **Track contributions to global needs.**
- Let the public see what fraction of a trillionaire's wealth is dedicated to solving hunger or water insecurity—compared to their asset growth.
- **Create a culture of stewardship.**
- Recognize those who step forward. Honor them publicly. And question those who choose to opt out.

Accountability isn't punishment—it's participation. Transparency isn't shaming—it's a **foundation for trust.**

3.4 Building the New Visibility

We do not need to vilify the ultra-wealthy. We need

to **illuminate them**—to make their roles, choices, and responsibilities publicly known.

Imagine a global dashboard showing:

- Each trillionaire's share of contribution toward ending hunger
- Real-time progress on clean water access worldwide
- Active humanitarian partnerships, deliveries, and impact zones

Imagine that dashboard becoming **as popular as the Forbes list**—but with a new ranking: not based on net worth, but **net human impact.**

This is not only possible—it is inevitable, if we demand it.

The trillionaire era is not just an economic reality. It is a moral challenge to civilization itself. Either we build the structures to ground power in responsibility, or we allow a new class of untouchables to float ever higher—while the rest of humanity drowns in need.

That's the choice. And the trillionaires will not make it for us.

A Turning Point in History

Every generation reaches a crossroads—one that reveals more about its values than any slogan, invention, or election ever could. For ours, that turning point is this: **we now possess the wealth to eliminate hunger and provide clean water to every person on Earth. But will we require it? Will we demand it?**

This is not a question of technical feasibility. The cost estimates are clear. The logistics are proven. Organizations like the World Food Programme, FAO, and UNICEF have mapped out the infrastructure. We know what it takes.

It's also not a question of available money. The trillionaire class—and even a fraction of the billionaire class—has more than enough capital to meet global sustenance needs multiple times over.

It's a question of **structure**. Of *will*. Of whether we believe that unprecedented wealth should come with unprecedented responsibility.

4.1 From Admiration to Expectation

Until recently, society treated the ultra-wealthy like folk heroes. We admired them. We ranked them. We put their names on buildings and tracked their net worths like box office scores. But admiration is no longer enough.

What we need now is **expectation**. Not resentment. Not blind adoration. But a rational, universal expectation that **if you have the power to end suffering, you are expected to do so.**

This shift has happened before. We once admired monarchs—until we demanded constitutions. We once admired robber barons—until we demanded taxes. Now, we admire tech giants and investor-industrialists—but it's time to demand **global civic duty**.

Expectations define civilizations. And right now, ours are too low.

4.2 Economic Evolution, Not Revolution

Some fear that holding the ultra-wealthy to global responsibilities will incite class warfare or economic collapse. That's a false binary. The proposal laid out in this book does not call for wealth seizure, punitive taxation, or ideological extremism. It calls for **structural evolution**.

Capitalism has evolved many times:

- With labor laws and minimum wage.
- With corporate taxes and social security.
- With international trade and environmental regulations.

We are simply proposing the **next logical step:** a built-in safeguard to ensure that the extreme wealth accumulating in a handful of hands also flows outward to meet humanity's most basic needs.

In short: this is not revolution. This is **redesign**.

4.3 The Moral and Legal Precedent Exists

Critics might argue that there's no precedent for requiring private individuals to assume global humanitarian roles. But in fact, the precedent is everywhere:

- **Mandatory military service** in many nations—when the stakes are national.
- **Universal taxation** based on income—not based on voluntary giving.
- **International law**, which holds war criminals accountable for acts against humanity, even across borders.

We have long accepted that **when power reaches a certain scale, it must be governed globally.** Nuclear weapons. Biological warfare. Now, **trillionaire economics** must enter that conversation.

The next frontier of international law is not just about weaponry or borders. It's about **wealth and its role in human survival.**

4.4 This Is the Moment

There will never be a more fitting moment than now:

- The first trillionaire is on the horizon.
- The climate crisis threatens food and water security everywhere.
- Global awareness of inequality has never been higher.
- Digital infrastructure enables worldwide transparency and accountability.

This book argues not only that we *can* create a system where the wealthiest are required to end hunger and provide water—but that **we must**, or we risk normalizing a new form of economic feudalism where unchecked wealth coexists with preventable suffering.

We stand at a turning point.

One path leads to a world where a handful live in gilded floating fortresses while billions struggle for bread and clean water.

The other leads to a future where **wealth becomes stewardship**, where those who have the most give the most—not by whim or PR, but by *design*.

That's the purpose of this book.

Not just to imagine that world—but to build it.

2

THE COST OF HUNGER
HUNGER BY THE NUMBERS

For most of the modern world, hunger is a word used more casually than it should be. "I'm starving," someone says before lunch. A skipped meal is treated as an inconvenience, not an emergency. But for **over 800 million people globally**, hunger isn't an exaggeration —it's a daily truth. It's malnutrition, wasted bodies, stunted development, and, for millions, an early death.

Hunger today is not due to a lack of food production. It's a failure of **distribution, infrastructure, and global political will.** There is enough food in the world to feed everyone. And yet, people die of starvation in countries where grain silos overflow just miles away. How did we let this happen?

This chapter explores hunger as a **measurable, solvable problem,** beginning with the facts that should haunt us— and move us to act.

1.1 Global Hunger Statistics: The Hard Truth

According to the **United Nations Food and Agriculture Organization (FAO),** as of the most recent reporting year, **roughly 9.2% of the global population is undernourished. That means one in eleven people does not consume enough calories to sustain basic health.

Of those, at least:

- **45 million children under age five** suffer from wasting (acute malnutrition),
- **148 million children** suffer from stunting (chronic malnutrition),
- And **millions more** suffer from micronutrient deficiencies that silently sabotage growth and brain development.

Every year, **more than 3 million children die from hunger-related causes.** That's over 8,000 per day. Roughly one child every ten seconds.

This is not due to famine alone. It's due to long-term poverty, interrupted food systems, poor sanitation, conflict zones, and neglect by both governments and the global economic order.

If a terrorist group killed 3 million children per year, the world would mobilize instantly. But when hunger does it—quietly, invisibly—it remains tolerated. This is the cruel arithmetic of indifference.

1.2 Regional Disparities: Where Hunger Hits Hardest

Hunger is not evenly distributed. While food insecurity exists even in wealthy countries like the United States (with over 30 million food-insecure individuals), the brunt of global hunger falls disproportionately on **Sub-Saharan Africa, South Asia, and conflict zones across the Middle East and North Africa.**

In Sub-Saharan Africa:

- More than **one-third of the population** faces food insecurity.
- Climate change, conflict, and supply chain collapses make even stable agriculture fragile.
- Rural areas often depend on rainfall alone, and when drought hits, entire communities face starvation.

In Yemen, Syria, Sudan, and the Horn of Africa, **war and displacement** have decimated farming systems and blocked food aid routes. In parts of Afghanistan, hunger rates approach **famine levels**, with winter starvation a recurring reality.

But even within countries, hunger targets the marginalized:

- **Women and girls** often eat last in patriarchal households.
- **Indigenous communities** are more likely to lack access to nutritious markets.
- **Children** suffer lifelong developmental delays when malnourished in their first 1,000 days.

Hunger is not just about empty stomachs. It's about broken systems that fail to deliver life's most basic necessity to those who need it most.

1.3 The Economic Cost of Hunger

Hunger does not just kill—it **drains economies, stunts growth, and perpetuates poverty cycles** across generations. According to the World Bank:

- Malnutrition causes a **10% loss in GDP** in

affected regions due to reduced productivity and higher healthcare costs.
- Stunted children grow into stunted economies. Cognitive delays, school dropouts, and lower lifetime earnings all follow.
- Every dollar spent on reducing hunger yields an estimated **$16 return in economic growth** through improved health, education, and productivity.

For example, in Southeast Asia, a large-scale nutrition program targeting rural children led to:

- Improved test scores in later schooling,
- Higher labor force participation rates in adulthood,
- And a measurable decrease in poverty rates 20 years later.

Hunger is not just a humanitarian issue. It is an **economic deadweight** that suffocates development, locks communities into desperation, and prevents entire nations from flourishing.

To solve it is not only to be moral—it is to be economically wise.

1.4 Beyond Calories: The Myth of Enough

It is also critical to understand that **hunger is not merely the absence of food**. Often, the issue is not quantity —but **quality**. This is called **hidden hunger**: a form of malnutrition where people have enough to eat in terms of calories, but not enough **nutrients, vitamins, or variety**.

- Diets based solely on rice, maize, or wheat provide energy but no resilience.
- Iron deficiency leads to anemia in over 1 billion people—especially pregnant women.
- Vitamin A deficiency causes blindness in children and increases infant mortality.

A child may eat a bowl of starch every day and still be starving.

This is why **food security must include access to diverse, nutritious, and culturally appropriate diets**, not just emergency rations or handouts. Hunger, when reduced to mere calories, can lull us into complacency. The solution must be rooted in **nutrition, dignity, and sustainability**.

The Long-Term Effects of Hunger

Hunger is not a momentary problem—it is a lifelong affliction. When a child is born into hunger, the consequences echo for decades. When a population lives in chronic malnourishment, the results stretch across generations, compounding poverty, illness, and inequality. Hunger is more than a lack of food—it's a biological trap.

This part examines the long-term effects of hunger on individuals, societies, and the trajectory of global development. It shows that hunger is not only a humanitarian emergency—it's a developmental catastrophe.

2.1 The First 1,000 Days: Lifelong Consequences

There is a period in every child's life—the first 1,000 days, from conception to age two—when the body and brain develop at an extraordinary rate. Nutrition during this time determines everything from **height, immune strength, cognitive ability**, to **long-term earning potential**.

Malnutrition during these first 1,000 days results in:

- **Stunted growth,** which affects one in four children under five in developing countries.
- **Impaired brain development,** reducing IQ and attention capacity.
- **Increased vulnerability to disease,** from diarrhea to pneumonia.
- **Lower educational attainment and lifelong poverty risk.**

Once this window closes, **many of the effects are irreversible.** A child who is malnourished at age two may never recover fully, even with later interventions.

The damage is not just physical. It's economic. It locks families—and entire communities—into **a multigenerational cycle of underperformance.**

2.2 Hunger and Education: A Mind Unfed Is a Mind Unformed

A hungry child cannot learn. Hunger impairs concentration, memory retention, and attendance. For children in extreme poverty, the cost of going to school while hungry is not just discomfort—it's failure.

In studies across East Africa, children in school feeding programs scored:

- **Higher in reading and math,**
- Had **better attendance,**
- Were **less likely to drop out** during the lean seasons.

For girls especially, access to nutritious food through school is often the **single factor that keeps them in education**—delaying marriage, increasing literacy, and reducing childbirth mortality rates.

Without nutrition, education becomes symbolic—a structure without substance.

And when education fails, so does every national aspiration for prosperity, innovation, and global competitiveness.

2.3 Hunger's Toll on Public Health

Chronic hunger is a quiet epidemic that weakens immune systems, burdens healthcare systems, and increases susceptibility to everything from infections to chronic disease.

- **Malnourished mothers** face higher risk of birth complications and maternal mortality.
- **Children weakened by hunger** are more likely to die from preventable diseases like measles or malaria.
- **Adults who grew up malnourished** are more prone to obesity, diabetes, and heart disease later in life due to metabolic disruptions.

Healthcare systems in low- and middle-income countries already face limited resources. Hunger **amplifies demand while reducing a population's ability to pay into that system.**

In essence, hunger is both a cause and a consequence of poor public health—and breaking that cycle requires not just clinics, but kitchens.

2.4 Hunger and Social Instability

Where hunger spreads, **conflict follows.** Not immediately. Not always visibly. But food insecurity erodes the social contract—fueling desperation, political unrest, and eventually violence.

Hunger drives:

- **Mass migration** from rural to urban centers, stressing infrastructure.
- **Recruitment into armed groups**, especially among young men with no jobs or purpose.
- **Food riots**, which have sparked revolutions and toppled governments.

The Arab Spring began in part due to rising bread prices. Venezuela's humanitarian crisis spiraled when food became scarce. Sudan, Syria, Lebanon—many of the world's geopolitical flashpoints are also **food insecurity flashpoints**.

Governments cannot rule empty stomachs. And societies cannot thrive on thin rations.

Hunger is not only a moral failing. It is a **national security threat**—one that transcends borders, ideology, and party lines.

It's Not a Supply Problem

The most haunting truth about global hunger is also the most absurd: **we grow more than enough food to feed everyone on Earth.** Every year, the world produces over 2.6 billion tons of cereal grains alone—more than enough to provide each person on the planet with over 2,700 calories per day.

And yet, hundreds of millions remain undernourished. Children die of starvation in a world that throws away nearly **one-third of all food produced.**

Hunger today is not about **scarcity**. It is about **systems failure**—logistical, political, and economic. The food is there. The problem is getting it to those who need it, when they need it, with the dignity and nutrition they deserve.

3.1 Global Food Waste: A Scandal of Abundance

According to the United Nations Environment

Programme (UNEP), nearly **1.3 billion tons of food** are wasted each year.

- In industrialized nations, most waste occurs at **the retail and consumer level**—uneaten meals, discarded produce, or unsold inventory.
- In developing nations, food waste often results from **lack of refrigeration, transportation, or storage.**

Food waste in Europe alone could feed **200 million people.** In the United States, discarded food equals about **$408 billion annually**, a figure larger than the entire GDP of many African nations.

And while this waste occurs, hunger persists.

This isn't just inefficiency. It's injustice. It's the failure of markets to serve moral ends, and the failure of policy to compel a better use of abundance.

3.2 Barriers to Access: The Infrastructure Gap

Food doesn't teleport. It moves by truck, ship, and plane. In regions where infrastructure is weak—roads unpaved, bridges unstable, ports inefficient—getting food to remote populations becomes nearly impossible.

- **Post-harvest loss** in Sub-Saharan Africa ranges from 15–35%, depending on the crop.
- **Seasonal rains** can wash out roads, isolating communities for months.
- **Power outages** mean refrigeration fails, and fresh food spoils before it can be consumed.

In conflict zones, food becomes not just inaccessible but weaponized. Humanitarian aid is blocked. Markets are disrupted. Civilians are besieged not with bullets, but with famine.

The solution to hunger, therefore, is not only farming more—it's **building the systems to distribute what already exists.**

3.3 The Price Problem: Food as a Commodity, Not a Right

Even when food is available, it's often priced out of reach. In many regions, rising food prices mean families must choose between **eating or educating a child, fuel or flour, medicine or maize.**

The **commodification of food,** driven by speculation, global trade policy, and profit motives, makes access precarious for the poor. Subsidies in wealthy countries can cause price distortions elsewhere. For example:

- U.S. corn subsidies lower global prices, hurting small farmers in Latin America.
- Grain speculation spikes prices even when harvests are abundant.
- Export bans during crises—like India's recent rice export restrictions—trigger panic in vulnerable importing countries.

In this system, food flows to **those who can pay,** not necessarily to those who **need.** The market rewards surplus and discards scarcity. The logic is economic. The consequence is **moral failure.**

3.4 Toward a Global Nutritional Justice Framework

To solve hunger, we need more than food banks and aid drops. We need a **global nutritional justice framework** that makes nutritious food:

- **Accessible** – through reliable transportation and local distribution systems.
- **Affordable** – with subsidies targeted at the consumer, not just the producer.
- **Culturally appropriate** – empowering communities to grow and eat foods aligned with their heritage.
- **Sustainable** – reducing waste, diversifying crops, and restoring soil and water systems.

We also need **funding at scale,** coordinated globally and enforced by law—so no one person or nation can turn their back on hunger while sitting on disproportionate wealth.

This is where the **Trillionaire Responsibility Model** becomes relevant.

The problem isn't food. It's will. It's logistics. It's allocation. And above all, it's the **lack of enforced, sustained global accountability** to fix what we already have the power to solve.

In short: hunger is not a supply issue. It's a **systems design issue**—one we can redesign, if those with the means are finally compelled to act.

The Political Cost of Starvation

Hunger is not merely a symptom of poverty or misfortune—it is often **a consequence of policy.** In the modern era, starvation can no longer be considered solely a natural disaster. It is frequently a **man-made crisis**—engineered, weaponized, or at the very least, tolerated for political gain.

Where food is scarce, politics thrives in the shadows. Where people are hungry, leaders bargain with bread. Hunger becomes a tool: **to suppress dissent, to reward loyalty, to manipulate populations, and to consolidate power.**

This part explores how starvation is wielded politically —and why any serious solution must include accountability, not just charity.

4.1 HUNGER as a Weapon of War

Throughout history, governments and armed groups have used food scarcity as a tool of warfare. In Syria, Yemen, Sudan, Ethiopia, and South Sudan, starvation has been deployed with ruthless precision:

- **Siege tactics** deprive entire cities of food and water to break resistance.
- **Aid blockades** prevent humanitarian access under the guise of security.
- **Resource pillaging** destroys farms and food stores as a way to punish civilian populations.

The UN recognizes **starvation of civilians as a war crime**, yet enforcement remains minimal. International condemnation often fails to translate into consequence.

In modern conflicts, hunger is no longer a byproduct—it is a **deliberate tactic.**

This makes solving hunger not only a logistical or moral issue, but a **matter of international peace and security.**

4.2 FOOD DEPENDENCY and Political Control

In authoritarian regimes or unstable democracies, food becomes **a means of control.** Governments may intentionally underfund rural food systems, withhold aid from opposition regions, or manipulate distribution to secure votes or compliance.

In Zimbabwe under Robert Mugabe, food was famously weaponized:

- Opposition supporters were denied food relief.
- State-run food programs became loyalty tests.
- International NGOs were restricted or expelled if their work undermined government control.

Similar patterns have occurred in North Korea, Venezuela, and parts of Myanmar.

When food is controlled by a central authority without transparency, it becomes **currency for control**—not sustenance for survival.

4.3 THE GLOBAL Politics of Inaction

Even in liberal democracies and affluent international organizations, **inaction is political.** Hunger persists not because we don't know how to solve it—but because solving it would require:

- Confronting corrupt governments,
- Challenging exploitative trade systems,
- And restructuring financial priorities that serve elite interests.

For example:

- Global military spending exceeds **$2 trillion annually**, while ending hunger would cost around **$50 billion per year**.
- Agricultural subsidies in wealthy nations distort

global food prices, making local farming uncompetitive in poorer nations.
- International food aid is often tangled in geopolitics—tied to donor preferences, branding requirements, and logistical conditions that delay or limit effectiveness.

This isn't a lack of funding—it's a **failure of prioritization.**

In many cases, global hunger exists **not because we can't fix it—but because those with power benefit from leaving it broken.**

4.4 Enforcing the Right to Food

The right to food is enshrined in:

- **The Universal Declaration of Human Rights (Article 25),**
- **The International Covenant on Economic, Social and Cultural Rights (Article 11),**
- And in numerous national constitutions.

Yet these rights are rarely enforced. There are no criminal penalties for governments or individuals who hoard wealth while others starve. There is no binding mechanism to compel those with surplus to support those in need.

This is why the **Trillionaire Responsibility Framework** proposed in this book is not just moral—it's political. It introduces a **mechanism of enforcement** where none exists. It reframes food security not as optional compassion, but as **required justice.**

When we say **hunger is political**, we mean that its solution must be too.

To change the system, we must not only fund food—but demand responsibility from those who are structurally positioned to ensure it.

Because if hunger can be engineered, so can its end. All it takes is the will to design a world where starvation is no longer tolerated—not by leaders, not by markets, and certainly not by those with trillions in their hands and nothing binding their conscience.

3

THE WATER DIVIDE

A *Hidden Global Emergency*
If hunger is visible—emaciated bodies, dry fields, empty bowls—then the global water crisis is its invisible twin. Water is everywhere and nowhere. We bathe in it, bottle it, pipe it, and irrigate with it. But over **2 billion people** worldwide lack access to **safely managed drinking water**, and over **4.2 billion** lack safe sanitation.

Unlike hunger, water insecurity is often less photographed, less televised, and less emotionally charged—perhaps because it is **so quietly lethal**. The pathogens in a glass of dirty water kill silently. The hours spent walking to the nearest well go unnoticed. The diseases linked to poor sanitation fester slowly, often out of sight of global headlines.

But make no mistake: **the global water crisis is one of the deadliest threats facing humanity.** And like hunger, it is solvable—if we make it a priority.

The Numbers That Shouldn't Exist

The **World Health Organization** and **UNICEF** define "safely managed drinking water" as water that is:

- Located on premises (not miles away),
- Available when needed,
- And free from fecal or priority chemical contamination.

Yet:

- **26% of the world's population** lacks access to this basic human right.
- **Over 800,000 people die annually** from diarrheal diseases directly linked to unsafe water, poor sanitation, and inadequate hygiene.
- **A child dies every 2 minutes** from waterborne illnesses.

These are preventable deaths. They are not caused by nature alone, but by broken systems, underinvestment, and international neglect. The water crisis is not new—it has just been **permitted to continue,** year after year.

Water and Poverty: A Vicious Cycle

Water insecurity traps families in a feedback loop of poverty:

- Time spent **fetching water**—often several hours per day—takes away from work, education, and caregiving.
- Lack of clean water leads to **illness,** which leads to **lost income,** which leads to **further marginalization.**
- Poor sanitation causes **absenteeism in schools,** especially for girls during menstruation, pushing them out of the education system entirely.

Access to water is not just about thirst. It's about **opportunity**. Without it, there is no time to learn, no strength to work, no chance to build a better future.

This is why the **United Nations recognizes access to clean water and sanitation as a human right**. Yet like so many rights, it remains aspirational for billions.

Why It Gets Ignored

Water is often called a "silent crisis" for a reason. It's not just that the deaths are spread out across time and geography—it's that the crisis rarely generates **public pressure**. Unlike dramatic famine or war, **water scarcity builds slowly**.

- Communities adjust to it.
- Governments underreport it.
- Aid agencies underfund it.

There is also an optics problem: **dirty water doesn't shock the Western eye** like a starving child might. Water isn't "marketable suffering" in the same way hunger is.

As a result:

- Funding for water initiatives **lags far behind** food relief.
- Infrastructure projects take a backseat to flashier aid campaigns.
- Solutions are often piecemeal, disconnected, or abandoned due to corruption or poor planning.

This must change.

Because the **human cost of water neglect** is not only unacceptable—it is entirely avoidable.

The Coming Storm: Population, Climate, and Collapse

Water insecurity is not just a problem for the Global South. It is a **growing global emergency**, accelerated by climate change, urban sprawl, pollution, and political mismanagement.

- By 2025, **half the world's population** is expected to live in water-stressed areas.
- Major cities like **Cape Town, São Paulo, and Chennai** have already experienced "Day Zero" scenarios, where reservoirs ran dry.
- Rivers like the **Colorado, Nile, and Yangtze** are shrinking or turning seasonal.

Water scarcity is **no longer a rural, developing-world issue**. It is arriving at the doorstep of megacities, destabilizing agriculture, raising tensions across borders, and threatening the food supply that depends on irrigation.

This is not a localized problem—it is a **planetary fault line**.

If the world does not act, we will see:

- Water wars.
- Mass displacement.
- Public health collapse on a scale even greater than hunger.

And yet, the world has the tools to prevent it—**if those with power and wealth are compelled to act.**

Infrastructure, Not Abundance

When people think of water crises, they often imagine **drought**—cracked riverbeds, dry reservoirs, parched land. But in truth, most places facing water insecurity **have water**. What they lack is **infrastructure**—the systems, technology, and governance to safely deliver clean water to the people who need it.

Access to water is not just about rainfall or natural supply. It is about **pipes, pumps, purification, and political will.**

The problem is rarely abundance. It is delivery. And without infrastructure, abundance becomes irrelevant.

THE IRONY of Proximity

In many parts of the world, water insecurity exists **within sight of the source:**

- Rural villages in South Asia are near rivers but lack purification.
- Communities in Sub-Saharan Africa live above aquifers but have no boreholes.
- Informal urban settlements may be adjacent to water mains, but are not legally connected to them.

This creates cruel irony: **people living next to water—but unable to drink it.**

They are left to fetch water from contaminated streams or open wells. They boil water with scarce fuel. They ration every drop, knowing that one illness could mean disaster.

In these cases, what's missing isn't water—it's **infrastructure investment and maintenance.**

THE GLOBAL INFRASTRUCTURE Gap

The **World Bank** estimates that the world would need to invest **$114 billion per year through 2030** to meet Sustainable Development Goal 6: universal access to water and sanitation. Currently, we're not even halfway there.

Many governments—especially in low-income countries—do not have:

- The capital to build systems,
- The technical expertise to design them,
- Or the governance stability to maintain them.

Even when systems are installed by NGOs or foreign governments, many **fail within 5–10 years** due to:

- Lack of local ownership,
- Maintenance neglect,
- Corruption or mismanagement,
- Political interference.

In Uganda, nearly **one-third of installed rural water points are nonfunctional** at any given time. In India, arsenic contamination seeps back into wells because mitigation was not built into the long-term planning. In cities from Lagos to Jakarta, failing infrastructure leaks up to **50% of treated water** before it reaches a tap.

We don't just need pipes—we need **accountable, funded, inclusive systems.**

Urban vs. Rural Divide

Urban areas often receive disproportionate attention and investment in water services, while **rural and peri-urban communities are left behind.** This widens inequalities:

- City dwellers may have piped access, even if unreliable.
- Rural families may walk for hours to hand-dug wells.
- Slum communities may pay more per liter from informal vendors than the rich pay for pressurized delivery.

Water becomes not just a service—but a **currency of privilege.**

This inequity isn't just geographic—it's structural. Infrastructure planning is shaped by politics, class, and profit. And when trillion-dollar fortunes are built from industries reliant on water-intensive production, while those in their supply chains go thirsty, **a moral failure becomes a logistical one.**

The Cost of Inaction

The costs of not building water infrastructure are staggering:

- In Sub-Saharan Africa alone, women spend **40 billion hours annually** collecting water—hours that could be used for education, employment, or rest.
- Inadequate water systems in healthcare facilities lead to **higher infection and maternal mortality rates.**
- Without sanitation infrastructure, open defecation contaminates drinking sources, perpetuating illness.

The ripple effects touch everything—health, productivity, education, dignity.

When we say that access to water is infrastructure-dependent, we mean this: **no amount of natural rainfall or aquifer depth matters if people can't safely access it.**

TRILLIONAIRE ACCOUNTABILITY in Infrastructure Development

Here lies a clear opportunity—and moral obligation—for the world's wealthiest.

Funding the infrastructure to deliver water and sanitation at scale is **not a charity campaign.** It's **a global human rights investment.** One that trillionaires could:

- Fully finance with negligible impact on their net worth,
- Support through public-private development partnerships,
- Accelerate using data-driven logistics and AI-powered system design.

Imagine a global system where:

- Trillionaires fund and oversee regional infrastructure hubs.
- Local communities are trained and employed to manage systems.
- International transparency dashboards track progress in real time.

With the **will,** it could happen.

What's missing is the **requirement**—the binding mechanism that says:

"If you possess the wealth of nations, you must help deliver the lifeblood of humanity."

Infrastructure is not glamorous. It doesn't make headlines. But it makes life possible.

Water without delivery is like food without access. It's useless. And too many lives are waiting on a pipe that never arrives.

Women and Water

To understand the true impact of the global water crisis, we must look not at the pipes, but at the people—especially the women and girls who bear the heaviest burden. In every region where water is scarce or unreliable, the labor of securing water falls overwhelmingly on **female shoulders**. And this burden is not merely physical—it is **economic, social, educational, and generational.**

Water scarcity is not gender-neutral. It is a **deeply gendered injustice**, affecting how girls grow up, how women survive, and how communities rise or fall.

WATER COLLECTION: **A Hidden Tax on Women's Lives**

Across the Global South, it is estimated that **women and girls spend a combined 200 million hours every day collecting water.** In countries like Ethiopia, Kenya, and Nepal, the average journey to fetch water may take **2–4 hours**, often across dangerous terrain.

This unpaid labor has staggering costs:

- Girls miss school or drop out entirely to assist with water collection.

- Women lose hours every day they could spend earning income, caring for children, or pursuing education.
- Physical strain leads to chronic pain, fatigue, and increased risk of complications during pregnancy.

The time lost is not just personal—it is **economic theft on a generational scale.**

Imagine if those 200 million hours were freed. Imagine the collective social, educational, and financial power of that shift. The impact would be transformative—not just for women, but for **entire nations.**

Safety and Vulnerability

For many women and girls, collecting water is not only exhausting—it is **dangerous.**

- The journey often takes them through isolated or conflict-prone areas.
- In refugee camps, slums, and rural zones, **sexual harassment and assault are common** at water points.
- In areas where conflict over water exists, women are caught between armed groups and violent disputes.

A 2020 study in South Sudan found that **nearly 1 in 4 women who collected water had experienced some form of violence** while doing so. Similar reports have emerged from displaced communities in Syria, Nigeria, and the Rohingya camps of Bangladesh.

And yet, these risks are often **underreported and normalized**. It's just part of daily life—for them.

Securing water should never come at the cost of **bodily autonomy or physical safety**.

MENSTRUATION, Sanitation, and School Dropout

For girls, the link between water insecurity and school dropout is especially acute during menstruation. When clean water and sanitation facilities are unavailable:

- Girls miss school for several days each month,
- Are subject to bullying or shame,
- And often **drop out entirely by age 12–14**, particularly in rural areas.

The absence of private, hygienic toilets affects not only their comfort—but their **dignity, confidence, and future**.

In India, a study by Dasra found that **over 23 million girls** drop out annually due to lack of menstrual hygiene management.

This isn't just about water—it's about access to opportunity, equity, and the ability to thrive without stigma or exclusion.

WOMEN AS WATER STEWARDS—BUT Not Decision Makers

Ironically, while women manage most household water tasks, they are **rarely included in decisions** about water systems.

- Women are underrepresented in water governance bodies.

The Trillionaire Club

- Water projects are often designed without community consultation.
- Technical training is typically offered to men, even when women perform the day-to-day maintenance tasks.

When women are included, the results improve dramatically:

- Projects are **more sustainable,** because women understand local needs.
- Water points are **better maintained,** because women have direct incentive to keep them operational.
- Systems are **better designed,** because they include hygiene and safety considerations often overlooked by male-only planning groups.

A 2010 World Bank report found that **water projects with female participation were six to seven times more effective** than those without.

The implication is clear: **Women must not only carry water—they must carry authority.**

Toward Gender-Responsive Water Justice

A truly just water framework must be **gender-responsive.** It must:

- Prioritize **women's time** and reduce the labor burden of water collection.
- Ensure **safe, accessible water points** close to homes and schools.

- Build **menstrual hygiene facilities** into all sanitation infrastructure.
- Guarantee **meaningful participation of women** in every step of water system planning and governance.

And most importantly, it must recognize water not just as a resource—but as a **human right that underpins women's empowerment and equality.**

Trillionaire responsibility must include not just the funding of pipelines, but the **design of systems that free women and girls from water slavery.**

What we build must liberate—not replicate—the burdens of the past.

Because a world where women still walk miles with jugs on their heads while billionaires discuss moon tourism is not a world of progress.

It's a world of profound moral failure—and a reminder that **water justice is women's justice.**

Men and Water

While the global water crisis disproportionately burdens women and girls in labor and safety, it also **shapes the lives, health, identity, and responsibility of men and boys**—in ways that are less visible, but deeply consequential.

Water is not just a domestic issue—it is a community, cultural, and ecological issue. In many parts of the world, **men control the political, economic, and agricultural systems that govern water**, while simultaneously being excluded from conversations about its day-to-day emotional and social dimensions.

Understanding men's relationship to water is essential to designing solutions that are **holistic, sustainable, and just.**

. . .

The Trillionaire Club

MASCULINITY **and the Politics of Water Ownership**

In many traditional societies, **water rights and land ownership are passed through male lineage.** Men make decisions about:

- Where water is allocated for irrigation,
- Which crops are grown,
- And which industries receive access in times of scarcity.

In these contexts, masculinity is linked with control over natural resources—and with the expectation to provide for one's family or tribe.

But water scarcity challenges this expectation. When rivers dry up, aquifers sink, or rain fails, men in agrarian communities experience **economic disempowerment.** Inability to provide—especially in patriarchal cultures—often leads to:

- Shame and social isolation,
- Increased substance abuse,
- Elevated risks of violence or coercion,
- Migration in search of opportunity, leaving families behind.

Thus, water scarcity fuels **male insecurity**, and in turn, social instability.

LABOR, **Risk, and Exposure**

In many water-insecure regions, **men perform the most dangerous water labor:**

- Digging wells in unstable ground,
- Repairing contaminated infrastructure,
- Operating heavy machinery without protective gear,
- Managing large-scale irrigation or flood management systems.

These roles expose men to physical risk, toxic chemicals, and chronic injury.

In mining, oil, and heavy industry—sectors with immense water needs—men often face **occupational hazards linked to poor water regulation**, such as:

- Waterborne skin and respiratory diseases,
- Long-term exposure to contaminated waste,
- Accidents in unstable or unsanitary conditions.

While women's water burdens are often domestic and invisible, **men's burdens often play out in public spaces, industries, and physical sacrifice.** They are different—but equally essential to recognize.

Disengagement from Domestic **Water Roles**

Culturally, water is often coded as a "female issue" in household and community life. This norm excludes men from:

- Household water planning,
- Hygiene and sanitation conversations,
- Caregiving tasks involving water—such as washing children or elderly relatives.

This disengagement perpetuates gendered labor inequality **and** limits community-wide water literacy.

When men are not trained in sanitation or do not value hygiene practices, entire families suffer. In some regions, **men may even sabotage water systems,** viewing them as unnecessary or challenging to traditional gender roles.

Reframing water as a **shared human responsibility**, not just "women's work," is key to sustainability.

WATER, Violence, and Peacebuilding

In fragile states and post-conflict zones, men are both the **primary combatants and peace negotiators** in water-related conflicts. When access is contested:

- Young men are often recruited into water militia groups.
- Elders and male leaders negotiate territorial or tribal water-sharing agreements.
- Male-dominated power structures determine how grievances are addressed—or ignored.

But men can also be powerful agents of peace.

Programs in Mali, Kenya, and Jordan have shown that when **men are included in water conflict resolution**, and are taught mediation rooted in sustainability rather than dominance, **tensions ease and cooperation rises.**

Water justice must therefore include **men as allies, not just actors.** It must:

- Acknowledge their vulnerabilities,
- Equip them to lead responsibly,

- And provide outlets for masculinity beyond control—such as stewardship, mentorship, and protection.

In short: water solutions must be gender-inclusive not just for equity—but for effectiveness.

Climate Change and Water Wars

The water crisis is not only a humanitarian issue. It is increasingly a **climate emergency**—and one of the most likely causes of **future wars.**

Water is the resource most directly affected by **climate instability.** As glaciers melt, rainfall patterns shift, sea levels rise, and droughts intensify, **freshwater sources are becoming unstable,** unpredictable, and in some places, unsalvageable.

The planet is not running out of water—it is running out of **safe, accessible, equitably distributed freshwater.**

CLIMATE'S IMPACT on Water Availability

Climate change is reshaping the global hydrological cycle in profound ways:

- **Glaciers,** which feed rivers in Asia, South America, and Europe, are shrinking rapidly. In the Himalayas, retreating glaciers threaten water access for **over 1.5 billion people.**
- **Rainfall patterns** are becoming erratic. Some areas now experience torrential floods followed by months of drought—making agricultural planning nearly impossible.
- **Groundwater depletion** is accelerating. The world's largest aquifers—like the Ogallala in the

U.S. or the Indo-Gangetic basin—are being pumped faster than they can recharge.
- **Saltwater intrusion** from rising sea levels is contaminating coastal freshwater systems, affecting countries like Bangladesh and island nations in the Pacific.

The result? Regions that once relied on stable water systems are now facing a **slow, irreversible collapse.**

WATER CONFLICT ZONES: **Past, Present, Future**
Water has long been a trigger for conflict:

- In the **Middle East,** disputes over the Jordan River and the Tigris-Euphrates basin continue to shape regional tension.
- In **Africa,** the Nile is a geopolitical flashpoint between Egypt, Ethiopia, and Sudan due to Ethiopia's construction of the Grand Renaissance Dam.
- In **Central Asia,** the retreat of the Aral Sea has fueled border tensions over irrigation rights and migration.

Future water wars may not look like traditional wars. Instead, they may take the form of:

- **Resource hoarding** by wealthy states,
- **Cyberattacks on water infrastructure,**
- **Privatization battles,** where corporations compete for ownership of water systems.

Without cooperation, the **competition for water** will define the geopolitics of the next century.

Migration, **Displacement, and Border Tensions**

Water scarcity is already driving migration.

In Guatemala, families leave farming regions where rainfall has vanished. In Syria, prolonged drought helped fuel the civil war by forcing rural families into cities, where economic collapse and ethnic tension ignited conflict. In sub-Saharan Africa, whole villages are moving inland as lakes dry up.

As climate change intensifies:

- Borders will become militarized.
- Refugee flows will rise.
- Cities will overflow with displaced populations.

And still, **the world lacks a comprehensive plan** to prevent this future—or to ensure that those who caused the least harm to the planet do not suffer the most.

Global Response or Global Collapse?

The world must decide:

- Will water be governed as a **shared planetary trust**, or will it be **monetized, militarized, and monopolized**?
- Will climate adaptation plans include **global freshwater protections**, or will each country fend for itself?

- Will we allow the wealthy to build luxury water access behind gates while the poor walk five miles to fetch mud?

Trillionaires—many of whom have built fortunes from water-intensive industries—must be held to account.

This isn't just about charity. It's about **climate justice, planetary security, and human survival.**

The time to act is not next year. It is now.

Because once rivers dry up, once aquifers are drained, once glaciers melt—they do not come back.

And the only thing more expensive than building water systems now is **fighting wars over them later.**

WATER AND HUMAN RIGHTS

The right to water is not a luxury. It is not a privilege of geography, income, or infrastructure. It is, quite simply, a **foundational human right—equal in importance to the right to life itself.** Yet despite decades of legal declarations and international consensus, billions of people still lack access to **clean water, nutritious food, and breathable air**—the very elements of survival.

This final part of Chapter 3 addresses water not just as a development issue, but as **a moral and legal imperative**—and situates it within the broader framework of **universal human rights.**

THE LEGAL RECOGNITION of Water as a Human Right

In **2010**, the **United Nations General Assembly** passed Resolution 64/292, which:

- **Explicitly recognized the human right to water and sanitation,** and
- Declared that clean drinking water and sanitation are essential to the realization of all human rights.

This resolution was followed by the **Human Rights Council Resolution 15/9**, which detailed the **obligations of governments** to ensure:

- Availability,
- Accessibility,
- Acceptability,
- Affordability, and
- Safety of water for personal and domestic use.

Despite these legal advances, the implementation has been weak. **Over 2 billion people still lack safe water,** and more than **3 billion lack basic handwashing facilities.** In practice, the "right" remains **aspirational—not enforceable.**

We have the language of rights, but not the **structures of accountability.**

THE TRIFECTA OF SURVIVAL: **Water, Food, and Air**

Human rights frameworks often prioritize civil and political liberties—freedom of speech, due process, the right to vote. But **what is the value of free speech to someone who cannot drink, eat, or breathe safely?**

The most fundamental rights are **biological.** They include:

- The right to **water**—to avoid thirst, disease, and death.
- The right to **food**—to avoid hunger, stunting, and physical decline.
- The right to **clean air**—to avoid respiratory illness and climate catastrophe.

Without these, all other rights are fragile. No court ruling or constitution can substitute for a body denied the elements of life itself.

This is why a truly **universal declaration of human rights in the 21st century must place water, food, and air at the center.**

Environmental Justice and Human Dignity

Denying someone access to clean water is not just a logistical failure—it is **an act of structural violence.**

- It forces mothers to give their children contaminated water, knowing it may sicken or kill them.
- It forces farmers to abandon land as their wells dry up.
- It forces children to spend hours hauling water instead of learning or playing.

This is not just a failure of policy. It is a denial of **dignity**—the foundational promise of all human rights frameworks.

Moreover, environmental justice cannot be divorced from **social and racial justice.** Across the globe:

- Indigenous peoples are displaced by water-intensive extraction industries.
- Black and brown communities suffer most from polluted water and inadequate sanitation.
- Low-income urban populations face privatized water systems that charge exploitative rates.

These patterns are not accidents. They are **systemic expressions of exclusion**, and they persist because rights remain unenforced for those without wealth or power.

The Responsibility of Wealth: From Recognition to Enforcement

The world's wealthiest individuals and entities exist within a system that **externalizes the cost of survival:**

- Bottled water empires extract from aquifers that leave communities dry.
- Industrial farming pollutes rivers while subsidized crop waste rises.
- Tech campuses and luxury homes in arid zones hoard water during historic droughts.

This is why the **Trillionaire Responsibility Framework** must be grounded in human rights law. It is not about philanthropy. It is not about generosity. It is about **legal and moral obligation.**

If water, food, and air are rights—and they are—then those with the means to secure them for all **must be required to do so.** The right to survive must not depend on **geography, income, or whether a billionaire chooses to care.**

Rights must be protected by **policy, contribution, and enforceable governance.**

TOWARD A DECLARATION of Planetary Rights

As we move forward into climate instability, population growth, and resource tension, the very concept of rights must evolve. We need:

- A **Universal Declaration of Planetary Rights,** recognizing the inalienable right of all people to clean water, food security, and breathable air.
- **Legal accountability mechanisms** that assign responsibility to states, corporations, and individuals—including those whose wealth could close the gap overnight.
- A **binding financial mandate,** wherein failure to ensure these rights results in automatic, proportionate contributions from those with extreme wealth.

Human rights without enforcement are empty promises. And water without governance becomes a tool of division, not survival.

This chapter ends with a call: Let us no longer treat water, food, and air as commodities to be purchased—but as **birthrights to be protected.**

Because in the end, if rights do not include the ability to live—they are not rights at all.

4

WHY CHARITY ISN'T ENOUGH
THE PHILANTHROPY PARADOX

In a world of escalating inequality, philanthropy often seems like the antidote. Billionaires launch foundations. Celebrities fund schools and water projects. Corporate giants announce donations during crises. Headlines trumpet generosity. Tax write-offs quietly follow.

And yet, despite this wave of high-profile giving, **global hunger, water scarcity, and poverty persist.** In some regions, they worsen. At the same time, the wealth of the world's richest individuals **continues to grow—sometimes even during economic recessions, pandemics, and disasters.**

This contradiction is not incidental. It reveals what we call the **philanthropy paradox:** a system in which enormous sums are given, yet **systemic injustice remains untouched,** or even deepens.

THE RISE of Mega-Philanthropy

In the last two decades, a new class of philanthropy has emerged: the **ultra-wealthy giving class.** Think:

- The Bill and Melinda Gates Foundation ($50+ billion),
- The Chan Zuckerberg Initiative,
- The Open Society Foundations,
- MacKenzie Scott's rapid-fire giving spree.

These philanthropists give more than some national governments spend on health and education. Their initiatives span everything from vaccines to education, sanitation to climate change.

And many do good work. They save lives. They innovate. They often act faster than governments can.

So why isn't it enough?

Because **philanthropy, by its very nature, is voluntary. It's unaccountable. And it's structured to preserve wealth and power—not disrupt it.**

Who Sets the Agenda?

When a billionaire donates $1 billion, it feels like a miracle. But in reality, that money often comes with:

- Conditions on how it's used,
- Preferences that reflect the donor's worldview,
- And limitations on long-term investment.

In short: **philanthropy allows the wealthy to play policymaker without running for office.** It substitutes public governance with private influence. It replaces democratic input with **boardroom consensus.**

Imagine if public health, education, or human rights policies were decided not by elected bodies or citizen advocates, but by **who signs the biggest check**. That's not a democracy—it's a plutocracy with better branding.

Billionaire-funded initiatives are not subject to the same accountability standards as public programs:

- No voter oversight.
- No independent auditing required.
- No guarantee of continuity or equity.

This creates a "**halo effect**", where donors are celebrated for acts that may be selective, self-serving, or inadequate—while deeper systemic change goes unaddressed.

STRATEGIC GIVING vs. Structural Justice

Philanthropy thrives on the idea of **"strategic giving"**—targeted, data-driven interventions that maximize short-term impact.

But solving global hunger, water scarcity, and climate degradation **requires systemic overhaul**:

- Redesigning global trade.
- Regulating monopolies.
- Holding governments and industries accountable.

These efforts are politically complex, slow, and often controversial.

Most philanthropists avoid them.

Why? Because strategic giving tends to:

- Avoid politics,
- Avoid confrontation,

- Avoid challenging the very systems that produced the wealth in the first place.

It's easier to fund a malaria net than fight the policies that made the malaria epidemic possible. It's easier to build a school than to question the privatization of public education. It's easier to write a check than to **share power**.

But unless the system is challenged, the crises return. And donors, no matter how well-intentioned, become **managers of crisis** rather than **agents of transformation**.

The Illusion of Enough

Finally, there's the issue of scale.

Even the most generous philanthropist cannot offset a trillion-dollar global shortfall with one-time giving. While a billion-dollar donation might sound massive, consider this:

- Ending global hunger would cost **$40–50 billion per year**.
- Delivering safe water and sanitation would require **$114 billion annually**.
- A single hurricane can cause **$100 billion in damages**.

Yet most foundations are structured to spend **only a small percentage of their endowment annually**—ensuring the capital remains intact while interest is used for grants.

This perpetuates **a slow-drip approach to massive emergencies**. It's the equivalent of applying a Band-Aid to a bullet wound while a vault of medical supplies sits untouched.

Charity can help—but **only enforcement, policy, and structural redistribution can truly solve.**

That's the central argument of this book: **philanthropy is not a substitute for accountability.**

Tax Avoidance vs. Public Good

While billionaires are celebrated for their generosity, their financial behavior often tells a more complex—and troubling—story. Behind the glowing press releases about grants and donations lies a global architecture of **tax avoidance, loopholes, and wealth preservation mechanisms** that dramatically undermine the very public goods philanthropy claims to support.

In many cases, the same individuals who give generously are also those who **extract disproportionately** from public systems while **contributing far less**—in taxes—than the average working citizen.

This part pulls back the curtain on the quiet war between **philanthropy and fiscal justice**, and shows how **systemic tax avoidance** undermines the moral legitimacy of charitable giving.

The Numbers Don't Lie

It is often assumed that billionaires pay more in taxes simply because they are wealthier. But the data reveals the opposite.

According to analysis by economists like Emmanuel Saez and Gabriel Zucman:

- The **average effective tax rate** paid by the top 400 wealthiest Americans is **lower than that of the bottom 50%** of households.

- Some billionaires pay **less than 1%** in taxes relative to the increase in their wealth, thanks to asset-based accounting, deferred taxes, and charitable deductions.
- A 2021 report by ProPublica showed that **Jeff Bezos paid zero federal income tax in multiple years,** despite his net worth surging by tens of billions.

How is this possible?

Because the ultra-wealthy don't earn income in the traditional sense. They own appreciating assets—stocks, real estate, equity in private companies—which are **not taxed until sold.** And many never sell.

Instead, they borrow against their assets to fund lavish lifestyles, investments, and yes—philanthropy.

This means that **charitable giving is often funded by wealth that has not been taxed—and may never be.**

Philanthropy as Tax Strategy

Charitable giving isn't just generous. It's often **strategically structured to minimize tax liability.**

When a billionaire donates to a private foundation, they can:

- **Deduct the donation** from their taxable income —often up to 60%,
- Retain **control over the foundation's assets,** board, and disbursement decisions,
- Invest the foundation's capital in ways that **continue to grow wealth tax-free,**

- And earn **social and political capital** in the process.

In many cases, the actual money reaching frontline service organizations is **a fraction of what is reported** as "given."

For example, a billionaire might donate $1 billion in company stock to a foundation:

- They deduct the full value for tax purposes,
- Avoid capital gains taxes on the stock,
- Retain voting rights over the stock while it's still in the foundation,
- And only disburse **5% annually**—the legal minimum required in many jurisdictions.

That's not charity. That's a **wealth management strategy.**

Public Goods Without Public Input

Meanwhile, public schools remain underfunded. Hospitals struggle with staff shortages. Water and sanitation infrastructure decays.

Why?

Because the revenue that should be available through **fair taxation** is instead locked in:

- Offshore accounts,
- Deferred asset gains,
- Tax-sheltered foundations.

The net result: **the public pays for its own**

poverty while applauding the wealthy for tossing down lifelines.

This creates a dangerous illusion: that the solution to poverty lies in the hands of the generous, rather than the **just**.

And when public services collapse, billionaires gain even more power—able to step in as saviors while their financial decisions helped weaken those systems in the first place.

SHIFTING the Narrative

The problem is not that the wealthy give. It's that **they aren't required to pay their share to the systems that support society.**

Philanthropy must not be used as a shield from taxation, nor as a substitute for democracy.

This is why the **Trillionaire Responsibility Framework** proposed in this book does not rely on charity. It proposes a **mandatory system** of contribution based on:

- Net worth thresholds,
- Global need forecasts,
- And enforceable, automatic obligations.

It does not ask the wealthy to choose when and how they contribute to the public good. It **requires it by law**, as taxation was always meant to.

Because clean water, food security, education, and health are not optional. And neither should the contributions be from those who benefit most from the global economic system.

Justice is not about voluntary generosity. It is about **structured responsibility.**

The Halo Effect

In today's media-saturated world, a large donation can do more than help a cause—it can **sanitize a brand, shield a reputation, and create a carefully curated image of moral virtue.** This is the **halo effect:** when public acts of generosity give wealthy individuals or corporations the appearance of benevolence, often deflecting scrutiny from the practices that generated their wealth in the first place.

The halo effect is powerful. It blurs the line between **justice and PR, impact and influence, accountability and applause.**

This part unpacks how the optics of giving have created **a new form of soft power** for the ultra-wealthy—and how that undermines genuine accountability.

Philanthropy as Public **Relations**

Major donations are rarely made in private. They come with:

- **Press releases,** media interviews, and viral hashtags,
- **Naming rights**—buildings, programs, scholarships,
- And often, **speaking opportunities and policy invitations.**

In return, philanthropists are lauded as visionaries. Magazine covers proclaim them saviors. Conferences give them the keynote. Documentaries feature their "impact."

This creates a public narrative: *look how much they give.*

But few people ask:

- *How much do they keep?*
- *How did they earn it?*
- *What systems remain unchanged beneath the donation?*

The result? Public perception becomes **distorted by visibility**. A billionaire who donates $100 million is viewed as more "moral" than someone who pays $100 million in taxes—though the latter supports schools, roads, hospitals, and public infrastructure **without controlling the outcome.**

Obscuring Harm

Some of the most celebrated philanthropists have also:

- Invested in industries that pollute water and displace communities,
- Underpaid workers or blocked unions,
- Profited from exploitative tech, labor, or housing markets.

Yet their donations to education or health initiatives create **moral camouflage**. They become heroes of reform—while avoiding the reform of their own business practices.

The most egregious examples include:

- Oil magnates funding environmental nonprofits,
- Surveillance tech billionaires supporting civil rights causes,
- Labor exploiters building vocational schools.

In each case, the donation draws the public's eye **away from the systemic harm.**

Philanthropy becomes **a reputational laundering machine**—cleaning the image while leaving the structure intact.

Celebrity Culture and the "Savior Narrative"

The halo effect isn't limited to billionaires. It thrives in the celebrity world as well:

- Movie stars visit impoverished villages for photo ops.
- Athletes launch charities that redirect attention from personal scandals or endorsements with unethical brands.
- Social media influencers brand themselves as activists without changing consumption patterns or business models.

The public, craving inspiration, embraces these figures. The media, eager for human interest stories, amplifies them. But the deeper structural issues—**the causes of hunger, water scarcity, inequality**—remain offstage.

This "savior narrative" keeps the public invested in the personalities of philanthropists, rather than the **policies that would eliminate the need for philanthropy in the first place.**

From Visibility to Accountability

So what would it look like to replace the halo effect with true **accountability**?

- Public dashboards tracking contributions relative to wealth—not just total donated.
- Transparency in business practices alongside donation records.
- Independent audits of foundation performance, not just feel-good metrics.
- And most importantly: **mandatory systems of global contribution** that don't rely on optics, applause, or personal branding.

The **Trillionaire Responsibility Framework** does exactly this. It ensures that the wealthiest don't just give—they **are required to contribute**, regardless of whether the cameras are rolling.

It asks: *What happens when the lights go off?* When there's no headline? No naming rights?

Real accountability means contributing **because it's right**, not because it's rewarding.

Because the world doesn't need more heroes. It needs more justice.

From Benevolence to Obligation

There is a long-standing belief in the global imagination that giving is a matter of **benevolence**—a private, voluntary act of goodwill. From religious tithes to modern foundations, charity has been praised as the pinnacle of moral behavior: the powerful choosing to help the powerless, the fortunate reaching out to the suffering.

But as we have shown throughout this chapter, that belief—while comforting—is no longer sufficient.

Voluntary generosity cannot replace structural justice. In a world of engineered inequality, climate disruption, and preventable death, the idea that help is optional is not only outdated—it is dangerous.

This final part of Chapter 4 calls for a paradigm shift: **from benevolence to obligation.** From gifts to guarantees. From saviors to stewards.

THE INJUSTICE of Optional Help

When solving hunger, providing water, or protecting the environment is left to the whims of the wealthy, we create a world in which:

- Survival is dependent on **charisma and connections,**
- Basic needs are met only when they align with donor interests,
- And rights are reframed as **favors.**

That is not equity. That is dependency.

Optional help reinforces the same power imbalance that created the problem. It says:

- *We will help you—if we feel like it.*
- *We will fix this—but only on our terms.*
- *We owe you nothing.*

This leaves the most vulnerable at the mercy of private timelines, private ideologies, and private distractions. What happens when a philanthropist loses interest? When a foundation changes focus? When a celebrity finds a new cause?

A rights-based world cannot rely on unpredictable generosity.

It must be **structured, sustained, and required.**

. . .

Reframing Wealth as Responsibility

The modern economic system is built on asymmetry:

- Global supply chains extract from poor nations.
- Tech and finance systems concentrate power in the hands of a few.
- Environmental degradation is driven by those who consume the most, while its effects are felt by those who consume the least.

In this system, **wealth is not neutral**. It is **relational, contextual**, and—when held in extreme concentrations—**morally consequential**.

To hold $1 trillion in personal wealth while children die from lack of nutrition or clean water is not just obscene. It is **unjust**.

The trillionaire class exists **because the system allows it**. And that system must now **require a return**—not as a punishment, but as a form of structural balance.

In the same way that we require corporations to pay taxes, drivers to carry insurance, or citizens to serve on juries, we must create **global obligations for the ultra-wealthy** that are:

- Proportional to their capacity,
- Tied to measurable goals,
- And enforced by international frameworks.

What Obligation Looks Like

Obligation is not vague moralism. It is **designed responsibility**.

Under the Trillionaire Responsibility Framework, reaching a trillion-dollar net worth triggers:

- **Automatic enrollment** in the Global Committee for Food and Water Security,
- **Mandated financial contributions** based on global need forecasts,
- **A surcharge mechanism** if global hunger or water insecurity targets are not met,
- And **transparent public reporting** of contributions, impact, and outcomes.

This is not an act of charity. It is a **contract with humanity**.

It says: *When you cross into extreme wealth, you become a steward—not a sovereign.*

It shifts power from private preference to **public responsibility**.

It transforms giving from an ego boost into **a civic duty** —one aligned with survival, equity, and sustainability.

THE END **of the Age of Applause**

For too long, we have clapped for billionaires who give while ignoring what they keep.

We have celebrated their generosity without asking about their taxes, their impact, or their business ethics. We have allowed a culture where applause substitutes for accountability.

That era must end.

We need a system where:

- The ultra-wealthy **cannot choose** whether or not to help end hunger.
- Every child's survival **does not depend** on a foundation's quarterly strategy session.
- The act of helping is not **extraordinary**, but expected.

Because in a just world, no one gets to opt out of humanity.

5
A NEW KIND OF OBLIGATION

Defining Ethical Wealth
The notion of **wealth as virtue** has deep roots in modern society. We tend to associate wealth accumulation with intelligence, discipline, and hard work. Billionaires are seen as innovators, disruptors, or saviors. Trillionaires will likely be elevated to near-mythical status —*economic deities* whose power stretches beyond borders and governments.

But the question we must ask now is not just how wealth is created—but **how it is wielded.**

In a world of finite resources, rising inequality, and widespread human need, **extreme wealth is no longer just a personal achievement.** It is **a global variable**—one that affects life expectancy, educational opportunity, climate adaptation, and human dignity across the planet.

The time has come to redefine what it means to hold extraordinary wealth—not simply as ownership, but as **obligation.**

. . .

From Personal Fortune to Global Impact

Let us first consider the scale of wealth we're talking about. A trillion dollars is:

- More than the GDP of most countries,
- More than the combined annual budgets of the World Health Organization, World Food Programme, and UNICEF,
- Enough to provide universal basic income in an entire region for a decade,
- And enough to feed every undernourished human being for **20 consecutive years.**

At that level, **wealth becomes infrastructure.**

It becomes power on a scale that rivals national governments and international agencies. But unlike governments, **there is no constitutional obligation**, no duty of care, no democratic oversight.

That must change.

We propose that **ethical wealth** at the trillion-dollar level must be defined by:

1. **Proportional responsibility** to global need,
2. **Transparency in contribution** to public good,
3. **Non-discretionary systems of giving** that scale with the wealth itself.

This is not about guilt or shame. It is about **structural fairness** in a global community.

Wealth in the Absence of Responsibility Is Violence

In 1967, Martin Luther King Jr. said, *"Philanthropy is*

commendable, but it must not cause the philanthropist to overlook the circumstances of economic injustice which make philanthropy necessary."

He might as well have been describing the 21st-century trillionaire.

When someone possesses enough money to end mass starvation, provide clean water to all, and reduce suffering at scale—and chooses not to—**that is not neutrality. It is negligence.**

Worse still, it's a form of **economic violence.** Because:

- Inaction maintains suffering.
- Hoarding resources amplifies global instability.
- And the very systems that concentrate wealth often **extract from those with the least.**

The ethical framing must evolve from:

- *"Look how much they gave"* to
- *"What is the cost of what they withheld?"*

This is why **ethical wealth must be grounded in contribution,** not just accumulation.

The Moral Case for a New Social Contract

The idea that wealth implies obligation is not new.

- In the ancient world, kings and landowners were expected to feed the poor in times of famine—or face divine judgment.
- In Islam, **zakat** (obligatory charity) is a pillar of faith, tied directly to wealth.

- In the post-war West, **progressive taxation** was considered patriotic, not punitive.

What we propose now is the **globalization of this moral logic**.
In a hyper-connected world, where:

- Capital flows across borders in milliseconds,
- Climate consequences affect every continent,
- And the ultra-wealthy have global reach—

We need a global ethic of wealth. One that is:

- Legally grounded,
- Morally coherent,
- And proportionally enforced.

That is the goal of the **Trillionaire Responsibility Framework.**

It transforms trillionaire status from a private milestone into a **public mandate**—from an ego achievement to a structural commitment to humanity.

Mandatory Responsibility Threshold

At the heart of this book's proposal lies a radical yet simple idea: **that reaching a trillion dollars in net worth should trigger a legal, binding obligation to contribute to the survival and dignity of the human race.** Not when convenient. Not when publicly advantageous. But always—and without exception.

This is what we call the **Mandatory Responsibility Threshold (MRT).**

It transforms wealth from an entirely private domain into a structure that comes with **public obligations, tied**

directly to the scale of that wealth. It is the ethical counterpart to global financial power—an operating principle that makes extreme accumulation contingent upon reciprocal contribution.

This part defines the MRT, explains how it works, and addresses the question many will ask: *Why now? And why this number?*

Why a Trillion?

The trillion-dollar threshold is more than symbolic. It marks a **paradigm shift in personal power.**

At this level, a single person:

- Can affect global food prices with a single investment.
- Has leverage over political parties, media ecosystems, and public perception.
- Can outspend entire governments on technology, logistics, and lobbying.
- May exert more influence on the future of humanity than heads of state.

A trillion dollars is not just personal wealth. It is **structural capacity**—a level of concentrated capital that can alter the trajectory of poverty, planetary collapse, or even civilizational survival.

Once a person crosses this threshold, they are **no longer merely an individual economic actor.** They become:

- A global stakeholder,
- A systems influencer,

- And a moral agent whose inaction has global consequences.

Thus, the trillion-dollar threshold must trigger a **global civic enrollment**—one that cannot be deferred, avoided, or negotiated away.

What Is the MRT?

The **Mandatory Responsibility Threshold (MRT)** is a legally codified trigger point at which:

1. A person's **net worth crosses $1,000,000,000,000 (USD)**, confirmed by internationally recognized financial disclosures or asset verification mechanisms;
2. That individual is **automatically enrolled** in the Global Committee for Food and Water Security (GCFWS);
3. They become subject to a **proportional contribution framework**, which allocates wealth toward solving hunger, water scarcity, and associated humanitarian crises;
4. Their participation is **transparent and enforceable** through international agreements, with tax-like penalties for non-compliance.

The MRT is not a tax in the traditional sense. It is a **global obligation structure**—an acknowledgment that at this scale of wealth, private freedom must give way to public duty.

. . .

Avoiding **Voluntarism and Opt-Out Culture**

One of the most toxic features of modern philanthropy is **voluntarism**—the ability to choose whether, how, and when to help.

Voluntarism enables:

- Selective compassion,
- Irregular commitments,
- PR-driven initiatives,
- And ultimately, **public dependence on private moods.**

The MRT eliminates that problem by **replacing personal discretion with systemic obligation.**

Once a person hits $1 trillion in verified net worth:

- There is no opt-out.
- There is no grace period.
- There are no exemptions based on nationality, citizenship, or domicile.

The threshold is **universal**, applying to all individuals globally who meet the criteria, regardless of where their assets are held or where they reside.

Built-In Flexibility, **Not Evasion**

To ensure the MRT is both **fair and functional**, it includes mechanisms that account for:

- Asset fluctuation (e.g., temporary net worth spikes),

- Long-term liquidity constraints (e.g., holdings in illiquid ventures),
- And macroeconomic conditions (e.g., systemic crises, currency devaluation).

However, these provisions are designed for **implementation**, not evasion.

For example:

- If net worth drops below the threshold for 12 consecutive months, participation in the committee may be paused.
- If asset liquidity is limited, individuals may contribute through equity stakes, infrastructure bonds, or convertible philanthropic investments.

But what they **cannot do** is:

- Declare offshore wealth as exempt,
- Revalue assets below market to avoid threshold,
- Or shift personal wealth into proxies to escape accountability.

Transparency, auditability, and enforcement are core to the MRT's credibility—and the next chapters will detail how that works.

Why Now?

The trillion-dollar wealth era is **no longer hypothetical**.

Financial projections suggest that within the next 5–10 years, we will see the first:

- Personal net worth crossing $1 trillion,
- Single individual with the power to close the hunger funding gap,
- Global response—or lack thereof—to this concentration of wealth.

To wait until this happens without a framework in place would be **to surrender the future to unregulated capital.**

The MRT is not just a financial mechanism. It is a **preemptive ethical firewall**—a safeguard that ensures humanity's most basic needs are never again subordinated to private indifference.

It is not about punishing success. It is about **redefining it.**

In a world where success means life for others—not just luxury for self—wealth becomes not a threat, but a blessing.

And that's the world we must now build.

From Rights to Responsibilities

In the modern era, we are taught to cherish **rights**—civil rights, human rights, consumer rights, the rights to speech, to privacy, to property. We inscribe these principles into constitutions, treaties, and charters. We consider them sacred. And we should.

But there is a dangerous imbalance when **rights are demanded without responsibilities**, especially by those whose wealth allows them to shape the world more than most governments can.

With great rights must come great obligations.

This section explores how the trillionaire threshold is not only a new economic milestone—it is a philosophical turning point. It represents a shift from a rights-based framework to one rooted in **reciprocity, duty, and global responsibility.**

THE AGE of Asymmetrical Power
Rights without corresponding responsibilities create **asymmetrical power structures**, especially in a globalized economy:

- Billionaires have the right to move capital anywhere in the world—but no binding responsibility to help the places they've extracted from.
- Corporations can assert intellectual property protections—but face no duty to ensure access to medicines or clean water in the developing world.
- The wealthy claim protection of privacy, investment freedom, and financial mobility—while the poor are bound by the rules of underfunded public systems.

This disparity allows power to become **detached from consequence**. It severs decision-making from accountability. And it leads to a world where **those with the most influence bear the least burden**.

The trillion-dollar club is the peak of this imbalance.

The Mandatory Responsibility Threshold corrects it— not by eliminating rights, but by tying them to **global civic duties**that scale with wealth.

REBUILDING the Social Contract
Every stable society is built on a social contract: an

understanding between the individual and the collective. In a just society:

- The citizen has rights—but also duties.
- The business has freedom—but also oversight.
- The wealthy have privilege—but also obligation.

The social contract is what makes civilization possible. It's why we pay taxes, follow laws, and contribute to public goods.

But the current global order has **broken this contract** for the ultra-wealthy.

At the trillionaire level:

- Wealth is largely untaxed,
- Contributions are voluntary,
- Influence is outsized,
- And obligations are nonexistent.

The result is **an invisible sovereign class**, above the rules of the game they continue to win.

The MRT restores the social contract at the top by saying:

- Yes, you may earn.
- Yes, you may invest.
- Yes, you may grow wealth.

But once that wealth reaches a trillion dollars, you must contribute proportionally to the survival of others.

Not out of guilt. Not out of shame. But because that is the contract required for the continued legitimacy of wealth itself.

Trillionaires as Global Citizens

The 21st century has created **a class of post-national individuals**. Their money moves seamlessly. Their businesses are borderless. Their influence transcends elections. But their responsibilities? They stop at the border.

It is time to declare that **trillionaire status carries with it global citizenship**—and that global citizenship requires:

- Stewardship of shared resources,
- Protection of public goods,
- And active contribution to planetary survival.

This is the moral extension of human rights.

If every person is guaranteed the right to food, water, and dignity, then those who hold disproportionate resources must be:

- Legally bound to help deliver those rights,
- Held to account when they fail,
- And honored when they fulfill that role faithfully.

This is not socialism. It is **sovereign-scale responsibility in a capitalist world**.

It asks: *If you can save millions of lives with a fraction of your wealth—why wouldn't you be required to?*

Reciprocity as Justice

The ethic of **reciprocity** is as old as civilization. It shows up in every major religious and moral tradition:

- *Do unto others...*
- *What you do to the least of these...*
- *The world is upheld by mutual care...*

In legal theory, it's called the **principle of fairness**: if you benefit from a system, you owe something back to it.

The ultra-wealthy have benefited from:

- Global supply chains,
- Government-funded infrastructure,
- Publicly educated workforces,
- Environmental resources they didn't create,
- And social stability they didn't pay to protect.

Reciprocity requires that this benefit be met with responsibility.

The MRT is **reciprocity codified**. It is **justice enforced**. It is the moral glue that turns raw capital into ethical wealth.

Without this shift—from rights to responsibility—our civilization cannot hold.

Fairness in a Global System

One of the first objections raised when responsibility is tied to extreme wealth is this: *"Why should I be penalized for success? Why me, and not others?"*

This question is rooted in a misunderstanding of **fairness**—a confusion between **equality of opportunity** and **equity of obligation**.

This final section of Chapter 5 addresses that objection directly and reframes fairness not as identical treatment, but as **proportional contribution based on capacity, impact, and benefit.**

Fairness does not mean we all carry the same load. It

means we all **carry what we can**—especially when others are carrying **more than they should** just to survive.

The Myth of Equal Responsibility

In the current global economy, responsibilities are distributed **inversely to power:**

- The poorest pay the highest percentage of their income in taxes.
- Low-income nations face crushing debt to institutions dominated by wealthier nations.
- Marginalized communities face the harshest effects of climate change, pollution, and hunger —despite contributing the least to the problem.

Meanwhile:

- Billionaires benefit from tax havens, regulatory gaps, and deferred capital gains.
- Multinational corporations externalize costs to workers, ecosystems, and developing countries.
- The ultra-rich live in fortified bubbles, insulated from the systems they erode.

This is not fairness. This is imbalance institutionalized.

The Trillionaire Responsibility Framework corrects that imbalance by tying contribution not to ideology, but to **capacity**—a principle already embedded in:

- Progressive tax systems,
- Means-tested services,

- And even religious tithe traditions.

We simply extend that logic to the global scale—and apply it to those at the top.

Trillionaire Contribution as Proportional Justice

Let's imagine two people:

- A worker earning $30,000 contributes 15% of their income through taxes, directly supporting schools, roads, and social services.
- A person with $1 trillion in wealth contributes 0.1% through optional philanthropy.

Who is truly contributing more?
Now imagine a system where:

- That trillionaire is required to contribute a portion of their wealth **in proportion to global need**—enough to feed millions, build water infrastructure, and invest in climate resilience.
- Their contribution is no longer exceptional. It is **expected**.

That is fairness.
Fairness means:

- Those who extract most from the system must reinvest most into it.
- Those who benefit most from globalization must sustain its future.

- Those who command the most resources must be **stewards**, not spectators.

This is not punishment. It is **proportional justice.**

ADDRESSING Global North vs. Global South
Fairness also requires confronting historical inequities between the **Global North and Global South.**

Most trillionaires—and billionaires—reside in or operate from wealthy nations:

- The U.S., Europe, parts of East Asia.
- Countries with strong legal protections, infrastructure, and access to global markets.

Yet many of their supply chains, labor sources, and resource extractions come from the Global South:

- Mineral wealth from Africa.
- Cheap labor from Southeast Asia.
- Agricultural inputs from Latin America.

The profits flow upward. The externalities remain. Fairness, in this global context, means:

- Wealth built on global systems must support global solutions.
- Food insecurity in Ethiopia, water scarcity in India, and sanitation gaps in Haiti are not distant problems—they are **symptoms of global design flaws** that benefit the few at the expense of the many.

To ignore that reality is not just unfair—it is **intellectually dishonest.**

A New Definition of Success

Ultimately, fairness in a global system means redefining what it means to be "successful."

Today, success is measured by:

- Net worth,
- Market dominance,
- Asset accumulation.

But what if we measured success by:

- **How many people were fed?**
- **How many communities gained clean water?**
- **How many lives were uplifted through fair and binding contribution?**

This is the ethos behind the **Trillionaire Club:**

- Not a private club of elites.
- But a **universal committee of stewards**, bound not by fame or fame, but by **responsibility to humanity.**

Fairness in a global system is not about capping ambition—it's about **anchoring it to justice.**

Because in a world of abundance, the failure to share is not a feature of freedom—it's a failure of civilization.

6

THE COMMITTEE OF THE WORLD

Automatic Enrollment
The core mechanism of the Trillionaire Responsibility Framework is more than a moral proposal—it's an institutional design. It does not rely on individual conscience or media pressure. It is **a structural guarantee,** made real through the creation of a standing, enforceable, and globally integrated governing body:

The Global Committee for Food and Water Security (GCFWS).

This committee is not theoretical. It is designed to operate **above partisan politics, beyond borders,** and **at the scale of global wealth accumulation.** And its first—and most revolutionary—principle is **automatic enrollment.**

This section introduces the architecture of the committee, beginning with how trillionaire participation is triggered and governed.

THE FAILURE of Voluntary Systems
To understand the need for automatic enrollment, we

must first recognize the deep limitations of voluntary global governance.

- International commitments (like the Paris Agreement) often lack enforcement mechanisms.
- Global summits issue declarations with no legal follow-through.
- Philanthropic commitments are made with no obligation to deliver—"pledged" dollars can remain unspent indefinitely.

In this vacuum, the wealthiest individuals have emerged as **sovereigns of influence**—free to act or not act, donate or divest, with **no systemic structure requiring their contribution.**

The Global Committee breaks this pattern.

It mandates that any individual whose verified net worth reaches or exceeds $1 trillion is automatically enrolled in the committee—without vote, without invitation, and without exception.

This removes discretion from the equation and ensures that **public responsibility is not left to private preference.**

TRIGGERING ENROLLMENT: A Transparent Process

Enrollment in the GCFWS is triggered through a **transparent, international asset verification process** governed by a coalition of:

- Global financial institutions (e.g., IMF, World Bank, BIS),
- National and regional tax authorities,
- Third-party audit bodies,

- And a UN-affiliated enforcement arm.

Once a person's net worth is certified to have exceeded the trillion-dollar mark:

- They are formally notified of enrollment in the committee,
- Their participation is entered into the **Global Public Registry of Stewardship**, a transparent online ledger,
- Their obligations under the Trillionaire Responsibility Charter begin immediately.

This process is not optional. It is embedded in international financial regulation, tax policy, and digital asset tracking infrastructure.

Just as corporations are subject to anti-money laundering laws or tax reporting requirements, ultra-wealthy individuals are bound to this participation requirement.

STATUS AND LEGAL **Standing of the Committee**

The GCFWS is not a think tank. It is not a symbolic advisory board. It is a **legal, enforceable committee with three distinct powers:**

1. **Mandated Strategic Duty:** Members are required to participate in goal-setting and resource allocation to eliminate hunger and provide clean water on a global scale.
2. **Financial Responsibility:** Members must contribute funds proportional to their verified net worth, based on annual cost projections

for achieving universal access to food and water.
3. **Transparency and Oversight:** Members' contributions, activities, and voting records are public—viewable by a global audience and subject to independent audit.

The committee operates under **UN-recognized international treaty law**, with signatory enforcement from nations and participation compliance built into global trade, financial, and diplomatic agreements.

In essence, the GCFWS is **a parallel structure of sovereign-scale responsibility**, created not to replace states, but to **hold individuals whose power exceeds most states accountable.**

TRILLIONAIRES AS TRUSTEES, **Not Tyrants**

The most radical element of automatic enrollment is this: **no one asks to join.** And no one can decline.

This sends a message to the world:

- That power of this scale is a form of **trusteeship**, not privilege.
- That reaching this threshold is not merely about personal success—it is about **planetary responsibility.**
- That the era of "self-made" detachment ends at a trillion.

To those who fear this erodes freedom: consider this—

- We already require service from those who serve in high office.
- We already require taxes from citizens.
- We already demand public disclosure from those in power.

What we propose is simply extending that standard upward—into the trillionaire stratosphere—where public impact is greatest, and current obligations are nonexistent.

Because if power is real, then so must be responsibility. And if wealth crosses all borders, then so must duty.

Committee Function

The Global Committee for Food and Water Security (GCFWS) is more than an elite circle of wealth. It is a **functioning global infrastructure mechanism**—designed to transform the concentrated capital of the ultra-wealthy into the **systems, solutions, and sustained funding streams** necessary to end hunger and water insecurity worldwide.

Its structure, powers, and procedures are not ornamental. They are **deliberately technocratic, legally binding, and globally coordinated**, ensuring that the committee is not just a symbolic gesture—but a working engine of justice.

This section details the **core functions** of the committee and how it operates across its three critical domains: strategy, funding, and delivery.

1. **Strategic Planning and Goal Setting**

The committee's first duty is **strategic visioning**—mapping out the annual, mid-term, and long-term priorities for global hunger and water elimination.

Each year, the GCFWS produces a **Global Access Blueprint (GAB)** which includes:

- Annual cost projections by region and crisis zone,
- Specific performance targets (e.g., reduction in undernourished children, rural sanitation installations),
- Risk mitigation plans (e.g., in conflict zones or fragile states),
- Partnership designations with NGOs, multilateral institutions, and public agencies.

These plans are created in collaboration with:

- The World Food Programme (WFP),
- UNICEF, FAO, and WHO,
- Regional water alliances and development banks,
- And frontline community-based organizations.

Trillionaire members are required to **participate in strategic sessions**, either directly or via designated delegates, ensuring their knowledge, logistical reach, and technological influence are applied to the public good.

The key principle: **no trillionaire remains passively enrolled. Each one must actively engage.**

2. Financial Contribution and Allocation

At the core of the committee's function is its financial engine. Every member is required to contribute **a proportional share of the total global funding target,** based on:

- Verified net worth,
- Number of active members,
- And current cost modeling of need.

For example:

- If global hunger and water infrastructure costs total $100 billion for a given year,
- And there are five trillionaire members,
- Each is assigned a base contribution of $20 billion,
- Adjusted by an equity-weighted multiplier that accounts for differential net worth and liquidity.

The system operates like a **public finance cooperative**, but at a planetary scale.

Contributions are held in the **Humanity Guarantee Fund (HGF)**—a UN-backed, independently audited, digitally tracked fund with:

- Zero tolerance for investment in fossil fuels, arms, or extractive industries,
- Full transparency via blockchain-based public ledgers,
- And automatic triggers for emergency disbursement during famines, climate disasters, or war-driven supply collapses.

This isn't donation. It's **duty-financed survival infrastructure.**

3. Oversight and Operational Execution

The GCFWS is not a delivery mechanism—it is an **oversight and financing body**. Its role is to fund, guide, and ensure accountability across a network of implementers. These implementers include:

- Global NGOs with decades of logistics experience (e.g., Médecins Sans Frontières, CARE, Oxfam),
- Governmental ministries for health, agriculture, and infrastructure,
- Local cooperatives and community-led organizations.

Key mechanisms include:

- **Performance-linked disbursements:** Funds are released in tranches tied to impact benchmarks (e.g., miles of pipe laid, meals distributed, wells installed).
- **Third-party monitoring and evaluation:** Independent agencies conduct real-time tracking of progress, with public reporting dashboards.
- **Sanction and clawback authority:** The committee can suspend funding to non-performing partners and reclaim misused funds.

In addition, **each trillionaire member is assigned a regional or thematic "stewardship domain"**—e.g., clean water in South Asia, child malnutrition in sub-Saharan Africa—ensuring active engagement in particular issue areas.

Participation is **not ceremonial**. It is managerial.

. . .

The Trillionaire Club

4. Emergency Activation Role

In times of acute crisis—famine, drought, pandemic, displacement—the committee may invoke its **Emergency Activation Protocol (EAP)**, allowing for:

- Rapid convening of virtual global sessions,
- Immediate liquidity infusion from the Humanity Guarantee Fund,
- Streamlined approval of mobile or aerial relief campaigns,
- Direct deployment of AI-predicted intervention zones based on real-time satellite and health data.

This positions the GCFWS as the **first responder of global capital**, capable of responding faster than any national government or traditional aid process.

Because in crises, speed saves lives. And speed requires **unprecedented prepositioned wealth**—the kind trillionaires hold.

A New Kind of Governance Body

In sum, the committee's function reimagines what governance can look like:

- Not beholden to electoral cycles,
- Not dependent on charity galas,
- Not trapped in the paralysis of geopolitics.

Instead, it is **wealth aligned with planetary responsibility**, guided by:

- Binding participation,
- Transparent contribution,
- Expert strategy,
- And direct impact.

It is what trillionaire wealth was meant to be: a tool of salvation, not speculation.

Rotating Governance & Public Oversight

Even the most ambitious systems of responsibility require more than good intentions—they demand **accountability, transparency, and participation.** Without these, any governing body—no matter how visionary—risks becoming an echo chamber, a tool of reputation management, or a vessel for elite self-interest.

To ensure the **Global Committee for Food and Water Security (GCFWS)** remains a legitimate force for global equity, it is governed by two essential structural principles:

1. **Rotating Governance** – No member dominates, no region monopolizes, and power circulates.
2. **Public Oversight** – Citizens, journalists, and civil society have eyes on every dollar, vote, and decision.

This section explains how these principles are embedded into the committee's charter, and how they ensure the committee remains a **public trust—not a private club.**

Rotating Leadership: Ending Perpetual Power

The committee operates on a **rotational leadership cycle**, structured around four key design features:

1. Annual Rotating Chair

- Every year, one committee member (or their designee) serves as **Chair of the GCFWS**, responsible for setting the strategic agenda, managing meeting cycles, and interfacing with global institutions (e.g., UN bodies, G20).
- No individual may serve more than once every 10 years.
- The rotation is **alphabetically randomized**, not wealth-weighted, to prevent dominance by any single member.

2. Regional Representation Guarantees

- The committee includes **regional advisory councils** composed of stakeholders from Africa, Latin America, Asia-Pacific, MENA, and Indigenous communities.
- Trillionaire members are required to **consult with these councils** when making strategic decisions affecting those regions.
- At least one advisory council member must be present for **all full-vote sessions**, ensuring **geographic diversity in decision-making**.

3. Issue-Based Co-Chair Rotation

- The GCFWS also rotates leadership by **issue domain**—water, food, hygiene, emergency response.

- These co-chairs are selected **not by wealth**, but by expertise, impact performance, and regional relevance.

This rotating structure ensures that **no single worldview, nationality, or ideology dominates the long-term direction of the committee.**
It institutionalizes humility—and blocks hegemonic capture.

Transparent Voting and Deliberation

Every major decision within the GCFWS—budget allocations, strategic priorities, emergency responses—is made by **deliberative vote**. The process is:

- **Recorded**, livestreamed, and published in full online.
- Accompanied by **member position statements**, which explain each vote.
- **Logged on blockchain**, ensuring **public immutability and auditability.**

To guard against informal backchannel collusion, the committee maintains:

- A **third-party ethics review board**, composed of civil society watchdogs, ethicists, and former heads of humanitarian agencies.
- An **AI-moderated conflict-of-interest engine**, which flags potential overlaps between member investments and proposed projects.

In short: every vote is tracked. Every interest is disclosed. Every action is subject to **real scrutiny**.

Because in the age of trillion-dollar influence, the **price of secrecy is collapse**.

THE PUBLIC DASHBOARD: Radical Transparency

Perhaps the most revolutionary tool of public oversight is the **GCFWS Public Dashboard**, a real-time, open-access digital platform that shows:

- Every contribution by every member—down to the dollar.
- Live implementation maps—wells built, meals delivered, systems installed.
- Third-party impact assessments—updated quarterly.
- Complaint and whistleblower submissions—automatically triaged to a public ombuds office.

The dashboard is:

- **Publicly funded**, not managed by any single member.
- Available in **every UN-recognized language**.
- Designed with **universal accessibility** in mind, including low-bandwidth versions for mobile and rural users.

This system gives the world what it has long lacked: **a clear window into power**.

It removes the mystique of wealth and replaces it with **data-driven truth**.

. . .

Citizen-Led Accountability Mechanisms

To further embed oversight, the GCFWS includes two innovative models of citizen participation:

1. The Global Citizen Jury

- Once a year, 50 citizens from around the world—randomly selected and demographically balanced—convene to review the committee's performance, interview members, and issue a **Citizen Performance Report.**

This report is:

- Public,
- Non-binding but **politically influential,**
- And included in every major policy forum the committee participates in.

2. Participatory Budget Allotments

- Up to **5% of the committee's annual budget** is allocated via **global participatory vote,** allowing everyday people to vote (via secure platform) on funding for specific innovations, regional projects, or emergency responses.

This feature reinforces the idea that **those affected by wealth should have a say in how it is used.**

Public Legitimacy Through Shared Power

By embedding **rotation, transparency, and public access**, the GCFWS doesn't just govern—it earns legitimacy.

It shows that trillionaire-scale responsibility is not about control—it's about service.

It proves that **power shared is power secured.**

It makes the wealthiest answerable to those they could once ignore.

And it ensures that the committee becomes **not just the regulator of hunger and water scarcity—but a model for how power can be justly structured in the 21st century.**

Enforcement Through International Treaty

Ideas are powerful. Institutions are impactful. But **only law makes obligation real.** Without legal enforceability, the most visionary frameworks are little more than proposals awaiting permission. That's why the Global Committee for Food and Water Security (GCFWS) is not just a philanthropic network or UN advisory body—it is rooted in a **binding international treaty**, ratified and enforced through global legal and financial systems.

This final part of Chapter 6 outlines how the committee's authority is legally codified and enforced across borders—ensuring that **no trillionaire can evade the obligations of planetary stewardship.**

THE GLOBAL TREATY on Trillionaire Responsibility

At the heart of the framework is the **Global Treaty on Trillionaire Responsibility and Resource Contribution (GTTRRC)**, adopted under the auspices of the United Nations and modeled after:

- The International Criminal Court (ICC) framework,

- The Paris Climate Agreement,
- And the International Treaty on Intellectual Property and Trade (TRIPS).

Key provisions of the treaty include:

1. **Mandatory participation upon net worth verification** of $1 trillion USD,
2. **Financial contribution enforcement** based on global humanitarian need forecasts,
3. **Asset transparency and reporting requirements** for compliance,
4. **Cross-border enforcement mechanisms**, including sanction triggers and reputational blacklisting.

Unlike soft treaties, which rely on voluntary compliance, the GTTRRC is designed to **integrate with national tax laws, banking systems, and trade protocols**—making non-compliance economically and diplomatically costly.

TREATY RATIFICATION **and Global Buy-In**

The GTTRRC is modeled to be compatible with national sovereignty while creating **supranational moral authority.** Nations are incentivized to sign and ratify the treaty through:

- **Access to GCFWS funding** for domestic hunger and water programs,
- **Preferential trade and financial partnerships** for treaty-compliant jurisdictions,

- **Public legitimacy and diplomatic prestige,** as participation signals a commitment to planetary equity.

Even countries whose citizens are unlikely to become trillionaires benefit by aligning with the treaty:

- They gain **access to infrastructure financing** through the Humanity Guarantee Fund,
- They are protected from global capital's worst extraction tendencies through treaty-aligned investment screening,
- And they share in the governance of an entity once reserved for elites alone.

By making this a **collective international covenant,** the treaty transforms trillionaire responsibility from private burden into **public mandate.**

SANCTIONS, **Penalties, and Enforcement Triggers**

To ensure compliance, the treaty establishes a tiered system of **enforcement tools:**

1. **Non-Compliance Taxation**

Trillionaires who fail to contribute according to their annual obligation are:

- Subject to a **global asset surcharge,** collected through participating nations' tax authorities,
- Assessed an additional **interest-based penalty** for each month of delinquency.

2. Reputational Blacklisting

Non-compliant members are:

- Flagged on the **Global Public Registry of Stewardship Failures,**
- Denied access to **global events, trade forums, and philanthropic tax deductions,**
- Publicly profiled in annual GCFWS failure reports.

3. Cross-Border Financial Restrictions

Member countries agree to enforce:

- **Freeze orders on non-compliant assets,**
- **Suspension of access to international credit markets and luxury asset registries,** including real estate, yachts, aircraft, and digital assets,
- **Provisional international warrants for asset disclosure** in severe, prolonged cases.

This suite of tools ensures that **being a trillionaire without contribution is more costly than compliance.**

Alignment With Existing International Law

The GTTRRC is designed to be **non-conflicting with existing treaties** and uses frameworks already recognized in:

- International financial regulation (via Basel III),
- Humanitarian law (via Geneva Conventions),
- Climate and human rights frameworks (via SDGs and Paris Accord).

The Trillionaire Club

This allows it to "plug in" to global institutions and operate across:

- G7 and G20 tax harmonization agreements,
- FATF (Financial Action Task Force) standards,
- WTO investment and trade rules.

Where existing treaties fall short, the GTTRRC fills the gap by creating a **direct path from wealth to obligation.**

FUTURE-PROOFING ENFORCEMENT

Finally, the treaty includes an innovative **Sunrise Provision,** which expands the scope of obligation as new thresholds emerge:

- If net worth thresholds increase (e.g., first $2 trillion individual), proportional increases in contribution are triggered.
- If emerging global risks (e.g., climate migration, pandemic food shortages) are declared by the UN, **emergency activation clauses** accelerate funding without further negotiation.

In this way, the treaty evolves with time—ensuring that no loophole, trend, or technicality undermines the **foundational principle:**
The greater the wealth, the greater the responsibility.

JUSTICE MADE **Law**

By rooting the committee's authority in international treaty law, the Trillionaire Responsibility Framework becomes more than a moral vision—it becomes **binding global policy.**

It transforms trillionaire status into a form of **civic service.**

It redefines citizenship at the highest economic level.

And it signals that in this new age of concentrated power, **no one is above accountability—not even the richest human on Earth.**

Because when survival is at stake, justice cannot be a suggestion.

It must be a law.

7

THE HUMANITY GUARANTEE FUND

Global Wealth for Global Survival
In a world driven by finance, it's no longer enough to envision a better future—we must **fund it**. While many global initiatives collapse under the weight of unfunded mandates, the Humanity Guarantee Fund (HGF) begins with the opposite premise: **funding comes first.** Outcomes follow.

The Humanity Guarantee Fund is the financial cornerstone of the Trillionaire Responsibility Framework—a purpose-built, enforceable funding mechanism designed to **convert extreme personal wealth into planetary infrastructure for food, water, and life.** It is not a bank. It is not a charity. It is a **perpetual global trust for the survival of the human species.**

In this part, we introduce the mission, design, and necessity of the HGF—and why nothing less will do.

Why a New Fund Is Needed

There are already thousands of aid organizations and

humanitarian programs. Billions of dollars flow through NGOs, UN agencies, and donor governments each year. So why create a new fund?

Because the existing system is **fragmented, slow, and structurally underfunded.**

- The **World Food Programme** often ends each year with **a billion-dollar shortfall**—despite growing hunger needs.
- **UNICEF's water and sanitation programs** routinely reach only **a fraction of target populations,** due to funding volatility.
- International aid budgets are subject to **national politics, recessions, and global crises**—as seen in COVID-19's decimation of humanitarian pledges.

Meanwhile, individual trillionaires accumulate more wealth **per month** than entire humanitarian systems do **per year.**

This disconnect reveals the truth: **we don't lack money. We lack structure.**

The Humanity Guarantee Fund fills that gap—creating a **predictable, enforceable, and permanently resourced mechanism** for delivering on the promise of universal food and water access.

FOUNDING **Principles of the HGF**

The Humanity Guarantee Fund operates on five core principles:

1. **Permanence**

The Trillionaire Club

- The fund is not campaign-based or temporary.
- It exists **in perpetuity**, backed by treaty and global financial regulation.
- It cannot be dissolved, privatized, or diverted.

2. Proportional Contribution

- All committee members (i.e., those exceeding the trillionaire threshold) contribute annually, based on:
  - A percentage of net worth,
  - The current global cost of hunger and water programs,
  - And equitable burden-sharing formulas.

3. Independent Stewardship

- The HGF is governed by an **independent, nonpartisan financial board**, composed of:
  - Global economists,
  - Auditors,
  - Public health experts,
  - And citizen observers (rotated annually by lottery from signatory nations).

4. Universal Benefit

- No country or population is excluded from HGF-funded programs.
- Priority is based on **need, not nationality**—ensuring the fund truly serves **humanity as a whole**.

5. Full Transparency

- Every contribution, investment, and expenditure is:
  - Publicly available in real time,
  - Auditable,
  - Linked to project outcomes,
  - And traceable via decentralized, open-source ledger technology.

These principles aren't idealistic—they are **non-negotiable**. They prevent corruption, ensure continuity, and create **institutional legitimacy** on a planetary scale.

Scope and Scale of Operations

The HGF is designed to operate with a **minimum annual baseline of $100 billion**, expandable to $500 billion in emergency years. Its use cases include:

- **Food Infrastructure:** storage, cold chains, supply chain optimization, community agriculture, school meals, food vouchers.
- **Water Access:** wells, filtration, desalination, sanitation, hygiene education, rain harvesting.
- **Systemic Capacity Building:** training local technicians, funding local governance, establishing regional resilience hubs.

Its funds are allocated not by donor preference, but by **regional need and strategic blueprinting**, updated annually through the GCFWS.

It also maintains **a 20-year sustainability reserve**,

allowing for long-term infrastructure maintenance, adaptation to climate shocks, and continuity through global recessions or conflict periods.

CURRENCY, **Custody, and Risk Management**
The HGF is not housed in a single currency, institution, or geopolitical region. It is designed to be **globally neutral, digitally integrated, and economically secure.**

Key mechanisms include:

- **Multi-currency reserve** in USD, EUR, CNY, and special drawing rights (SDRs).
- **Decentralized digital custody** across 12 host countries, preventing single-point political capture.
- **Risk insurance and reinsurance coverage**, underwritten by treaty-aligned firms.
- **AI-driven forecasting**, simulating geopolitical, commodity, and climate risk models to guide fund deployment and reserve strategy.

Every dollar is protected. Every investment is ethical. Every outcome is linked to **human life and dignity.**

NOT A DONATION—**A Guarantee**
Perhaps most importantly, the HGF is not described in moral terms. It is not:

- A "charitable cause,"
- A "passion project,"
- Or a "strategic gift."

It is a **guarantee**—a financial covenant between the richest people in history and the rest of humanity.

It promises:

- That no child will starve while a trillionaire exists.
- That no village will drink disease-ridden water while extreme capital sits idle.
- That no government will plead for funds when global capital could respond faster than famine spreads.

This is the new contract.

And the Humanity Guarantee Fund is how we sign it.

Fund Governance and Safeguards

For the Humanity Guarantee Fund (HGF) to succeed, it must do more than pool wealth—it must **earn trust**. Trust from the public. Trust from governments. Trust even from those required to fund it. This trust cannot come from sentiment, image, or ideology. It must come from **unshakable governance**—designed not just for operational excellence, but for transparency, protection, and fairness.

This part details how the HGF is governed: who controls it, how decisions are made, what safeguards prevent abuse, and how the world holds it accountable.

THE HGF BOARD OF TRUSTEES: **Independent and Unbribable**

At the heart of the HGF is its **Board of Trustees**, a 21-member body empowered to:

- Approve fund disbursements,

- Monitor global need assessments,
- Oversee legal compliance,
- And protect the fund from interference—private, political, or institutional.

Key characteristics of the board include:

1. **Diverse Global Representation**

- Each continent nominates 2 board members through a rotating, multistakeholder process involving national governments, NGOs, and academic institutions.
- 5 members are appointed by **citizen lottery**— randomly selected, vetted, and trained community leaders from low- and middle-income countries.
- No more than 2 members may come from nations represented by trillionaire funders.

2. **Financial and Ethical Expertise**

- At least 10 board members must have demonstrable credentials in:
  - Global finance,
  - Audit and compliance,
  - Public health systems,
  - Or ethics and human rights law.

3. **Term Limits and Transparency**

- Terms are fixed at 5 years with no immediate reappointment.
- All decisions are:

- Livestreamed,
- Recorded,
- Published within 48 hours with annotated minutes.

There are **no private boardrooms**, no off-the-record lobbying, and no closed-door fund manipulation.

Three-Tiered Safeguard Model

To prevent corruption, failure, or collapse, the HGF uses a **three-tiered safeguard model:**

Tier 1: Structural Design Safeguards

- **No individual or nation can withdraw or dissolve the fund.**
- All assets are **split across multiple jurisdictions,** and legal custodianship rotates every 2 years.
- Major disbursement decisions require a **supermajority vote (70%)** from the Board of Trustees.

Tier 2: Third-Party Monitoring and Audit

- The fund is **externally audited** annually by:
  - One UN body (e.g., UNDP or WHO),
  - One independent multinational firm,
  - One rotating public university audit team.
- Audits are published in full and linked to **live budget dashboards** available to the public.

Tier 3: Global Citizen Oversight

- An elected **Public Ethics Council (PEC)**—composed of journalists, civil society leaders, and investigative researchers—reviews:
  - Complaints against the fund,
  - Conflict-of-interest claims,
  - And allegations of underperformance or misuse.

The PEC has the power to:

- Freeze disbursements,
- Recommend board dismissals,
- Trigger an international review tribunal (through UN legal mechanisms).

This creates **a checks-and-balances loop** so that no actor, no matter how wealthy or well-meaning, operates above scrutiny.

Political Neutrality **by Design**

A key danger of any global fund is **political capture**. To prevent this, the HGF is structured to remain **neutral, apolitical, and agenda-proof:**

- It **cannot fund political campaigns, military interventions, or police equipment.**
- It **cannot enter trade or investment contracts** that include private lobbying clauses.
- Board members, staff, and contractors are banned from holding office or corporate board seats **within 5 years of service.**

In addition:

- **Languages, currencies, and media platforms** used by the fund rotate annually to prevent Euro-American cultural dominance.
- Every regional office has **independent hiring authority**, removing central political or cultural gatekeeping.

This neutrality ensures the fund works for **the world—not for donors, host countries, or ideologies.**

SAFEGUARDING **Against Technological Overreach**

As the fund relies on advanced digital infrastructure—AI forecasting, blockchain auditing, biometric verification—safeguards are also in place to:

- Prevent surveillance misuse,
- Protect vulnerable populations from data exploitation,
- And prohibit fund-related platforms from being monetized or privatized.

All HGF data systems are:

- **Open source**, reviewed annually by international transparency watchdogs,
- **Federated**, meaning no single server, company, or government controls the full data ecosystem,
- And stored with **algorithmic ethical firewalls**: smart contracts that prevent funds from being

allocated to harmful uses (e.g., surveillance, debt traps, carbon-intensive infrastructure).

Technology is a tool—not a tyrant.

A Fortress Built on Public Trust
The Humanity Guarantee Fund must be more than solvent. It must be **untouchable in integrity**. Because when the survival of millions rests on a bank account, there can be **no shadow, no slush, no scandal**.

It is a fortress—not because it protects wealth, but because it protects lives.

And it is built not on capital—but on **consent, design, and unflinching transparency**.

Ethical Investment and Deployment Strategy

While the Humanity Guarantee Fund (HGF) is primarily a humanitarian instrument, it also serves as a **financial engine**—not just to hold funds, but to **grow and deploy them strategically** for sustained global impact. This dual role introduces both opportunity and risk: capital can compound, but it can also corrupt. The solution is a deliberate architecture of **ethical investment protocols and precision-targeted deployment strategies**, ensuring every dollar of growth serves life, not speculation.

This part explores how the HGF builds wealth without moral compromise—and deploys it with impact, speed, and justice.

Principles of Ethical Investment
Unlike sovereign wealth funds or private capital

markets, the HGF follows a **triple mandate** for its asset portfolio:

1. **Preserve principal for long-term humanitarian continuity.**
2. **Grow capital through low-risk, ethical investments.**
3. **Deploy liquidity aggressively during crises or extreme need spikes.**

But all investments must align with **ethical screens** rooted in global justice. The fund may **not** invest in:

- Fossil fuel extraction or deforestation,
- Weapons manufacturing or surveillance technology,
- Speculative food commodities,
- Private water monopolies,
- Or any entities known to violate labor, environmental, or human rights standards.

The fund **does** prioritize investments in:

- Green infrastructure,
- Regenerative agriculture,
- Sustainable water tech,
- Community-driven health solutions,
- And socially responsible bonds.

These screens are enforced by:

- A permanent **Investment Ethics Panel**, composed of experts from finance, ecology,

human rights, and indigenous wisdom traditions;
- Annual public reporting of **portfolio composition and ESG compliance;**
- A global advisory portal allowing **civil society organizations to flag concerns.**

No investment exists purely for yield. Every dollar must pass the test of **human dignity and planetary stewardship.**

PORTFOLIO STRATEGY and Global Risk Mitigation

The fund's investment portfolio is diversified to withstand market shocks and systemic crises while maintaining:

- **80% capital preservation and humanitarian liquidity goals,** and
- **20% mission-aligned growth strategies.**

To mitigate regional instability, currency crises, and political risks, the fund:

- Holds assets in a **distributed global trust architecture** across multiple currencies and jurisdictions;
- Employs **AI-based scenario modeling** to predict risk up to 5 years in advance (e.g., war zones, resource collapse, inflation);
- Maintains a **climate-adaptive investment rotation,** withdrawing from water-intensive regions or carbon-exposed industries during stress periods.

This isn't reactive giving. It's **adaptive investment with an ethical spine.**

Crisis Liquidity Protocols

In times of acute emergency—famine, flood, displacement—the fund's **Crisis Liquidity Protocol (CLP)** is activated.

Key features:

- **Automatic pre-approved disbursement thresholds** based on mortality risk or infrastructure collapse forecasts,
- **Pre-positioned cash equivalents and digital transfer rails** (e.g., mobile payments, emergency food credits),
- **Zero-delay contracting with regional implementation partners** who meet ethical certification and have proven logistical readiness.

The CLP is governed by:

- A rapid-response subcommittee with 72-hour decision authority,
- Oversight by UN-coordinated disaster response task forces,
- Live-streamed transparency dashboards so **the world sees every dollar in motion.**

This ensures that when catastrophe strikes, the response is **measured in minutes, not months.**

. . .

DEPLOYING FOR SYSTEMS, **Not Symptoms**
Unlike traditional charity models, which treat symptoms (a meal, a bucket, a medicine drop), the HGF prioritizes **systems-based deployment**, funding projects that:

- Build **permanent clean water access**, not temporary bottled deliveries;
- Strengthen **community agricultural infrastructure**, not short-term food drops;
- Enable **local ownership**, training, and employment, not extractive contract relief.

Examples of funded projects:

- Solar desalination and water harvesting cooperatives in rural sub-Saharan Africa,
- Cold-chain food hubs and logistics networks in Southeast Asia,
- Regional seed banks and agroforestry zones in Latin America,
- Urban sanitation innovation labs and circular water systems in densely populated megacities.

Deployment is **decentralized but data-integrated**—each regional office has budget discretion based on real-time need scores, but all data feeds into the Global Access Blueprint (GAB), ensuring:

- Accountability,
- Outcome benchmarking,
- And participatory evaluation by local stakeholders.

. . .

EQUITY FIRST: **Deployment by Urgency and Injustice**
All fund deployment is governed by the **Equity First Allocation Model**—a tri-layer rubric that determines priority based on:

1. **Urgency** – populations currently facing hunger, malnutrition, or contaminated water;
2. **Historical Injustice** – regions disproportionately impacted by colonization, extraction, or systemic underdevelopment;
3. **Systemic Vulnerability** – areas likely to face compounding risk from climate change, political collapse, or economic exclusion.

This means the fund does **not** prioritize based on:

- Media attention,
- Political leverage,
- Donor interest,
- Or short-term metrics.

It prioritizes based on **justice**—and it does so transparently.
Every dollar deployed can be:

- Tracked in real-time,
- Cross-referenced by location and outcome,
- Audited through open-access records.

WEALTH REIMAGINED as Regenerative

In this system, wealth is not hoarded or symbolic. It is **regenerative**.

A trillionaire's contribution becomes:

- A pipeline to a village,
- A hot meal for a child,
- A water system for a school,
- A training program for local engineers.

And as investments grow, their returns **re-seed the fund** —perpetually.

This is not trickle-down economics. It is **circle-up stewardship**—a closed loop where capital moves, grows, and returns **in service of humanity.**

The End of Excuses

For centuries, the great injustices of the world have been justified by excuses—excuses rooted in complexity, scarcity, sovereignty, or scale. Leaders have said: *"It's not possible." "It's not affordable." "It's not our job."* But the creation of the **Humanity Guarantee Fund** ends all of that.

It doesn't just make hunger and water scarcity solvable —it makes them **inexcusable.** Because once the money exists, and the structure exists, and the enforcement exists, **so does the obligation.**

This final section of Chapter 7 isn't just a technical close. It's a moral declaration. A line in the sand between **the age of indifference** and **the age of planetary responsibility.**

THE LAST OBSTACLE Was Always Will—Not Wealth

We've long been told that global hunger and water insecurity are **tragic but inevitable.** But the math was always wrong:

- The cost to end world hunger? $50 billion/year.
- The net worth of the first trillionaire? Likely to exceed $1,000 billion.
- The wealth held by the top 1%? Over **half the world's total assets.**

In other words, **we could have solved these problems decades ago.**

What stopped us was not money. It was the **lack of a binding mechanism** to connect that money to the problems it could solve.

The Humanity Guarantee Fund eliminates that gap. It removes the last excuse. It says:

- You have enough.
- You are obligated.
- You can no longer look away.

Because from this point forward, **not contributing is no longer morally neutral**—it's morally bankrupt.

Justice Without Permission

For too long, justice has waited on permission—permission from donors, from voters, from markets, from media attention.

The HGF flips that script. It **does not ask permission. It requires contribution.**

It doesn't care whether:

- A trillionaire feels inspired today.
- A government wants to align this year.
- A hedge fund is in the mood to play nice.

It operates on **law, not lobbying.** It moves on **fact, not favor.**

And it applies not just to today's trillionaires—but to those still coming. **It sets a precedent** for how power must be governed in the age of hyper-concentration.

What Excuses Still Remain?

Let's name and dismiss the most common objections:

"It's too complicated."

No, it's not. The technical tools exist. The legal pathways are modeled. The institutions are ready. It's not complexity —it's cowardice.

"It's not fair to penalize success."

It's not a penalty. It's proportionate stewardship. When you hold more than entire nations, you don't get to pretend you're a passive observer. You are a participant. You are an agent. You are accountable.

"Private wealth is private business."

Not when it affects the public good. Not when inaction leads to death. Not when that wealth is built on public infrastructure, labor, environment, and extraction. **Extreme wealth is never just personal.** It's structural.

"Someone else should act first."

No more deferrals. No more passing the buck. The world is burning. The children are hungry. The water is contaminated. The first person with a trillion dollars must act. And so must the second. And the third. **There is no one else.**

. . .

This Is the Threshold of a New Civilization

With the Humanity Guarantee Fund, the world finally has a blueprint for **what ethical civilization looks like in the 21st century.**

Not slogans. Not speeches. **Structures.**

Not goodwill. **Accountability.**

Not dreams. **Deployment.**

The fund is not the end of the road. It is the foundation for what comes next:

- Climate justice finance.
- Health security infrastructure.
- Education as a planetary right.

But none of that matters if we can't feed each other and keep each other alive.

That is the baseline. That is the floor. That is the promise.

There Are No More Excuses. Only Decisions.

Every generation reaches a moment when excuses expire. This is that moment.

Because when trillions are hoarded and children are hungry, the moral math is clear.

Because when clean water is just a pipe away—and the money exists to lay it—inaction is betrayal.

And because **if we can build rockets to Mars,** we can build pipelines to villages.

The question is no longer *"Can we afford it?"*

It's *"Can we live with ourselves if we don't?"*

8

CASE STUDIES FROM THE FUTURE
THE LAST MILE IN NORTHERN KENYA – WATER COMES TO GARISSA

Date: July 18, 2032
Location: Garissa County, Kenya
Population Impacted: 274,000
Trillionaire Contributor: Meera Shah (Founder, SolGrid Tech)
Funding Stream: Humanity Guarantee Fund – East Africa Water Portfolio

BEFORE THE FUND

For generations, residents of Garissa—a dry, arid region in northern Kenya—survived on seasonal rains and shallow wells. During drought years, which became more frequent as the climate changed, children walked **6 to 10 kilometers per day** to find water—often from stagnant pools shared with livestock. Cholera outbreaks were seasonal. School attendance plummeted. Women lost entire days to water gathering. And when the droughts stretched beyond two seasons, **livelihoods collapsed entirely.**

NGOs came. They dug boreholes. Some broke. Others ran dry. A few lasted—but only in towns close to roads.

By 2025, more than half the region's population was classified as **water-insecure**, and nearly 60% of deaths under age five were **linked to waterborne illness or dehydration-related malnutrition**.

That year, Meera Shah became the world's third trillionaire.

And everything changed.

THE INTERVENTION BLUEPRINT

Upon automatic enrollment in the **Global Committee for Food and Water Security**, Shah was assigned **stewardship of East African rural water systems**. Her initial contribution to the Humanity Guarantee Fund was $22.8 billion.

Of that, $1.02 billion was immediately allocated to the **Northern Kenya Hydration Corridor Project**—a system of:

- Solar-powered desalination and borehole hybrids,
- Gravity-fed pipeline networks reaching 84 rural clusters,
- Regional maintenance and repair training schools,
- Water ATM kiosks where users tap prepaid credits tied to universal digital IDs (free for low-income residents).

The intervention began in 2026 and was completed in just under six years.

What changed?

The Trillionaire Club

. . .

WHAT IT LOOKS Like Now

It's 2032. The dusty red clay of Garissa is still hot. But everywhere you look, there are signs of a **revolution powered by water.**

1. **The Walking Has Stopped.**

Girls who once spent 4 hours per day collecting water are now in school. Water kiosks—solar-powered and digitally managed—are located every 500 meters, with maintenance crews available 24/7. "We used to walk past bones in the dry season," says Asha, a teacher. "Now we walk our children to class."

2. **Cholera Is Functionally Eliminated.**

No new outbreaks have been reported since 2029. With safe water, handwashing infrastructure, and latrine-linked greywater systems, hygiene has become normalized. "We haven't seen the emergency clinic filled with sick children in three years," says Dr. Kibwana at the Garissa Regional Hospital.

3. **Jobs Have Appeared.**

The pipeline network and kiosk system created 1,120 permanent jobs—technicians, software operators, sanitation educators. Youth unemployment in the district has dropped by 42%. "I fix pumps. I teach my daughter about pressure valves. It feels like we matter now," says technician Yussuf Ali.

4. **Water Ownership Has Shifted.**

The system is now governed by a local cooperative. HGF funded the buildout but mandated **local control and accountability.** The community elects a management board every three years, and digital dashboards show every drop dispensed, every repair request, and every kiosk's uptime—on display in schools and mosques.

The Human Impact

Before the fund:

- Infant mortality due to dehydration: **23.4 per 1,000 births**
- Annual school dropout rate (girls): **35%**
- Average hours/day spent gathering water: **3.8**

After the fund (2032 data):

- Infant mortality due to dehydration: **1.9 per 1,000 births**
- School dropout rate (girls): **4%**
- Average hours/day spent gathering water: **0.2**

"Water is not our prayer anymore," says local elder Farah Noor. "It's our birthright."

How It Was Funded, Audited, and Sustained

- Meera Shah's contribution was traced through the **Humanity Guarantee Fund ledger**, publicly viewable by anyone with a smartphone.
- The project's cost projections, benchmarks, and KPIs were updated in real time via the GCFWS deployment dashboard.
- Local contractors were trained and certified through the **Ethical Water Builders Program**,

created by the fund to ensure **no external labor dependency.**

Meera Shah was not praised with statues or titles.
But she **was held accountable**—and she **delivered.**
Not because she's kind.
Because she **had to.**
Because the system made it **non-optional.**
Because **global survival is not a donation.**
The Urban Food Grid in Dhaka, Bangladesh – Feeding 10 Million With Dignity
Date: October 1, 2033
Location: Dhaka, Bangladesh
Population Impacted: 10,200,000+
Trillionaire Contributor: Rafael Moreno (Global Retail Platform Founder)
Funding Stream: Humanity Guarantee Fund – South Asia Urban Hunger Initiative

THE PROBLEM: **A City on the Brink**
By the late 2020s, Dhaka had become one of the most densely populated cities on Earth. Home to over 20 million people and growing, it suffered from:

- Soaring food inflation,
- Erratic monsoon crop failures,
- A rural migration surge caused by coastal sea level rise,
- And a deeply fragmented supply chain choked by congestion and corruption.

In 2026, nearly **1 in 4 residents** of Dhaka reported skipping meals for entire days. Food riots were not uncommon. Markets were overrun during rice deliveries. Infants were born underweight, and teenage girls sold ration cards to pay rent.

The problem wasn't absence of food—it was **access, logistics, and dignity**. People didn't just need calories. They needed a **system**.

That same year, Rafael Moreno—founder of the largest global e-commerce and logistics firm—crossed the trillion-dollar net worth mark. Upon automatic enrollment in the Global Committee for Food and Water Security, he was assigned to the **Urban Hunger Portfolio – South Asia**.

His mission: redesign food access in megacities from the ground up.

THE INTERVENTION: **Dhaka Urban Food Grid (DUFG)**

Beginning in 2027, the **DUFG** was funded with an initial $3.6 billion contribution from Moreno's obligation under the Humanity Guarantee Fund. The intervention had five components:

1. **Digital Subsidy Platform**

- Every resident below the poverty line was issued a **biometrically linked food credit account**, usable at any certified vendor.
- Credits were dynamically adjusted based on inflation, household size, and medical need.
- No cash required. No bribery risk. No humiliation at handouts.

2. **Cold Storage Micro-Hubs**

- 158 **urban micro cold chains** were installed within slums, industrial zones, and transportation hubs.
- Food waste dropped by 48% in the first year due to spoilage reduction.
- Local farmers gained direct access to the city, bypassing exploitative middlemen.

3. Mobile Food Vending Fleet

- Electric tuk-tuk-style vendors, run by trained youth cooperatives, delivered fresh produce and protein across underserved zones.
- All vendors were GPS-tracked, safety-audited, and connected to a public pricing algorithm to prevent price gouging.

4. Women-Led Urban Farming Cooperatives

- Over 10,000 rooftops were converted to micro-farms, supported by fund grants and solar irrigation.
- Female-led co-ops were paid market rates through smart contracts tied to nutritional diversity benchmarks.
- Domestic violence rates dropped by 11% in neighborhoods where co-ops formed.

5. Real-Time Hunger Mapping and Response

- The city installed a **food insecurity dashboard** using mobile phone survey data,

satellite imagery, hospital malnutrition reports, and AI-driven predictive modeling.
- Crisis zones received immediate inventory rerouting or price intervention authority from the GCFWS Dhaka Response Cell.

The Transformation

By 2033, ten years after the start of the DUFG, the transformation was evident on every street:

- **Children eat before school, not after work.**
- **Food prices remain stable** even when the monsoon floods rail lines.
- **Farmers now sell directly to city aggregators,** earning 2–3x more per kilo of produce.
- **Shame is gone**—replaced by autonomy, mobility, and participation.

Rahima, a 39-year-old mother of four in the Kamrangirchar district, said it best:

"Before, we begged for lentils. Now we pick from five shops and ask about protein content. My daughter says she wants to be a nutritionist. Can you imagine?"

Measurable Outcomes (2033)

After (2033)

Undernourished Population
27%

4.3%
Average Daily Meals (low-income adults)
1.3
2.7
Food Vendor Coverage
2.1 per 10,000
14.8 per 10,000
Urban Food Waste
36%
14%
Monthly Food Riots
2–3
0 (since 2030)
All improvements are documented on the GCFWS-Dhaka Public Impact Dashboard, updated every 24 hours and available in Bangla, English, Urdu, and Hindi.

A TRILLIONAIRE **Without a Crown**
Rafael Moreno was not invited to ribbon-cuttings. His image does not appear on food kiosks. No branding. No plaques. No vanity.

Because this is not philanthropy.
It's obligation.
Enforced by law.
Guided by equity.
Driven by systems—not saviors.
His reward is not applause.
It's that **10 million people are eating tonight.**
The Resilience Zone in the Amazon Basin – Indigenous Stewardship and Water Sovereignty
Date: February 9, 2034
Location: Upper Rio Negro, Brazilian Amazon

Communities Impacted: 342 Indigenous villages across Brazil, Colombia, and Venezuela

Trillionaire Contributor: Tahlia Winslow (Crypto-Mining Executive Turned Regenerative Financier)

Funding Stream: Humanity Guarantee Fund – Amazon Resilience & Water Justice Portfolio

BEFORE THE FUND: Collapse by Extraction

For decades, the upper Amazon basin—home to some of the world's most biodiverse ecosystems and most historically marginalized Indigenous peoples—was under siege. Logging, mining, river pollution, and unsanctioned dam construction had:

- Contaminated vital waterways with mercury, lead, and arsenic,
- Displaced entire tribes from their ancestral territories,
- Introduced chronic waterborne illness and food insecurity into once self-sufficient communities.

By 2028:

- 43% of children under age 5 in the Rio Negro region showed signs of stunting or malnutrition,
- Water from 6 out of 10 tributaries tested unfit for human consumption,
- Entire cultural and linguistic groups were at risk of extinction due to forced migration and ecological collapse.

All while the region's deforestation helped fuel the

fortunes of global commodities firms and digital currency processors requiring intensive energy and land access.

Ironically, it was the rapid expansion of crypto-infrastructure that pushed Tahlia Winslow to the trillion-dollar mark. Upon her automatic enrollment in the **Global Committee for Food and Water Security**, she was assigned the **Amazon Basin Regenerative Mandate**.

She asked no questions. The law was clear.

She paid in full.

THE INTERVENTION: The Amazon Resilience Zone (ARZ)

From 2029 to 2034, over $5.8 billion was allocated from Winslow's HGF contribution toward the creation of the **Amazon Resilience Zone**, the world's first **bioregionally governed, Indigenous-led food-and-water security corridor**.

The ARZ was not built *for* Indigenous communities. It was built **by** them.

Core Components:

1. Water Sovereignty Trust

- 19 river systems were declared **non-commodified water commons**, with legal title and governance ceded to tribal federations recognized under the ARZ treaty.
- Filtration and monitoring nodes were installed at strategic points, powered by micro-hydro and solar arrays.
- Every village received an emergency safe-water cache tied to satellite weather prediction systems.

1. Forest Food Infrastructure

- Agroforestry systems were expanded using native crops (cassava, açaí, cupuaçu), supported by eco-certification and market integration channels to sell goods globally.
- Canoe-and-drone distribution networks connect 200+ communities with regional hubs—ensuring dry season resilience and cultural continuity.

1. Decentralized Biohealth Stations

- 86 clean-water clinics were established, combining Indigenous medicinal knowledge and modern waterborne disease prevention protocols.
- Each facility includes water chemistry labs, oral rehydration centers, and water literacy education hubs—staffed and governed by locals trained through the **Water Keepers Fellowship**.

1. Digital Land and Water Registry

- A blockchain-based registry records **ancestral territory claims, water rights, and pollution violations.**
- Backed by legal authority of the GCFWS and regional courts, the registry has already prevented 64 illegal land grabs and triggered 11 successful ecological compensation claims.

What Life Looks Like Now (2034)

In the village of São Gabriel da Cachoeira:

- Young girls collect spring water not from muddy edges, but from a **stream node** that glows green when safe.
- Elders review **real-time mercury levels** from their village dashboard.
- Teenagers log bird calls on solar-powered tablets that also transmit water flow data to the GCFWS.

No one waits for aid.
They **own the system.**

Outcomes (2028 vs. 2034)

Villages with access to safe year-round drinking water
21%
93%
Child stunting prevalence
43%
8.7%
Incidence of mercury poisoning
19 cases/month
0 in 16 months
Annual displacement due to water or food insecurity
3,200+
< 100
Regional youth migration rate
17%
4%

These numbers are not abstract. They are lived.
And they're published, audited, and verified through the

GCFWS Bioregional Dashboard, translated into Tikuna, Baniwa, Yanomami, and Portuguese.

THE END of Extraction Without Accountability
Tahlia Winslow never returned to the basin in person. Her wealth once drew power from its rivers.
Now, her responsibility **repaired** them.
Because that's what the Humanity Guarantee Fund demands:

- Not a favor. A function.
- Not sympathy. **Sovereignty.**

This is **the post-extraction world.**
And it begins with clean water—owned by those who protect it.
From Desert to Harvest – Yemen's Food Transformation
Date: May 4, 2035
Location: Al-Hudaydah, Taiz, and Ma'rib Governorates, Yemen
Population Impacted: 7.1 million directly, 14.5 million indirectly
Trillionaire Contributor: Li Wen (AI Agritech Industrialist, East Asia)
Funding Stream: Humanity Guarantee Fund – Middle East Food Stability Portfolio

THE PROBLEM: **Hunger in a Land of War and Salt**
Yemen, a nation scarred by a decade of war and geopo-

The Trillionaire Club 145

litical proxy conflicts, was for years synonymous with **humanitarian despair:**

- Over 80% of the population required food assistance by 2025,
- 2.3 million children suffered acute malnutrition,
- Agricultural infrastructure lay in ruins—bombed irrigation canals, salinized soils, and fractured rural economies.

International donors came and went. Blockades continued. Delivery routes were unsafe. Hunger was weaponized. Relief was politicized. And ordinary families endured starvation in silence, living on **bread, tea, and fear.**

By 2028, UN officials were calling Yemen *"a famine of human engineering."*

The conflict faded. But the hunger **remained**. Until the world's fifth trillionaire—**Li Wen**—was enrolled in the Global Committee for Food and Water Security.

Her mission: **Build the largest post-conflict food restoration program in recorded history.**

THE INTERVENTION: **The Yemen Food Sovereignty and Green Growth Plan**

Beginning in late 2028, Li Wen's $11.3 billion obligation under the Humanity Guarantee Fund was partially routed to Yemen—specifically to rebuild the entire food system under the **Food Sovereignty and Green Growth Plan (FSGGP).**

Core Components:

1. **Solar-Powered Seawater Agriculture**

- Coastal desalination plants were built to power inland drip systems and **halophyte agriculture**—growing crops in salt-impacted soils using brackish water.
- Farmers grew quinoa, barley, and date palms in previously unfarmable zones.

1. **AI-Guided Irrigation Cooperatives**

- Over 1,200 farming cooperatives were launched across Ma'rib and Taiz, using AI sensors to monitor soil health, evaporation rates, and planting cycles.
- Yield increased 3–5x, while water use decreased 40% compared to traditional flood methods.

1. **Women-Led Agricultural Training Corps**

- Nearly 80,000 women were trained as agronomists, crop monitors, seed conservators, and educators—many of whom were war widows or displaced persons.
- Social capital was restored through **land restoration and food distribution roles.**

1. **Mobile Desert Markets**

- Electric caravans linked rural farmers to regional cities via a solar-powered cold chain, drastically reducing food spoilage and price instability.
- All prices were stabilized by GCFWS algorithmic fair market tools, ensuring that **profit didn't come from scarcity.**

1. **Nutritional Revival Centers**

- Community kitchens were established across 17 districts to combat malnutrition with **locally grown food**, therapeutic feeding, and culturally dignified care—managed entirely by local councils, funded by the HGF with **zero military or political intermediaries.**

TRANSFORMATION: **Fields Where There Were Graves**
In 2035, the change is unrecognizable.
In Al-Hudaydah:

- Children eat before school, and school gardens are linked to daily lunches.
- Families who once survived on food rations are now **food exporters**, selling halophyte grain blends to regional buyers.

In Ma'rib:

- Tribal leaders who once fought over wells now sit on the same **Agricultural Water Council**, mapping rainfall catchments and AI-predicted crop rotations.

In Taiz:

- Teenagers are growing hybrid vegetables for both consumption and seed conservation—and dreaming of careers in **botanical AI design.**

"Where my father was shot, my daughter now plants," says Amal Al-Qadhi, a mother of five and now lead trainer at the Women's Farming Union in Ibb.

Outcomes (2028–2035)
National undernourishment rate
55%
12%
Average daily calories available per person
1,220
2,650
Female agricultural workforce participation
6%
39%
Number of functioning cooperatives
47
1,237
Rate of food imports
78%
32%
Perhaps most astonishing: Yemen now exports **water-stable grain hybrids and resilient seed stock** to other water-scarce nations in the region.
The **desert has become a teacher.**

When Repair Becomes Policy
Li Wen did not build this system out of benevolence.
She built it because she **was obligated.**
Because the Humanity Guarantee Fund left no room for excuses.

Because *"too complicated"* and *"too broken"* were no longer acceptable answers.

Today, Yemen is not merely fed.

It is **sovereign.**

And every grain of rice grown without fear is a reminder:

Justice is not charity. It is policy—finally made real.

9

ACCOUNTABILITY WITHOUT BORDERS
THE DIGITAL LEDGER OF STEWARDSHIP

In the old world, wealth existed behind walls—hidden in trusts, foundations, offshore accounts, and symbolic gestures. Accountability was sparse, data was siloed, and the public had to rely on **journalists, whistleblowers, and investigative NGOs** to uncover truth from shadows.

Not anymore.

The Trillionaire Responsibility Framework created something radical: a **Digital Ledger of Stewardship (DLS)** —a real-time, tamper-proof, open-access system that allows any citizen on Earth to **see what the wealthiest people in the world are doing with their responsibility.**

This isn't surveillance. It's transparency—**at scale, at speed, and in service of the public good.**

What the Digital Ledger Is—and Isn't

The **Digital Ledger of Stewardship (DLS)** is a:

- **Global transparency architecture**, maintained and protected under a UN-backed digital treaty framework;
- **Immutable financial record**, built on next-gen blockchain technology that logs every transaction, commitment, delay, and impact related to the Humanity Guarantee Fund;
- **Public dashboard interface**, accessible via web, mobile, radio-encoded transmission (for offline areas), and even **audio-only networks** in rural and underserved communities.

The DLS is not:

- A tracker of personal purchases, private consumption, or lifestyle behavior;
- A political profiling tool;
- Or a crowd-shaming platform.

It does not exist to punish wealth. It exists to **verify contribution**—to turn **responsibility into visible, trackable, moral infrastructure.**

How It Works: Three Core Data Channels

The ledger operates across **three interoperable channels,** each representing a distinct layer of accountability:

1. **Contribution Channel**

- Logs each trillionaire's verified net worth (updated quarterly),
- Calculates required annual contribution (based on formula from Chapter 5),

- Records when, where, and how that contribution is made (cash, equity, bonds, infrastructure, emergency reserves),
- Flags **late, partial, or missing contributions** in red, auto-generating public alerts.

2. Allocation Channel

- Shows how funds are distributed across geographies, program types, and urgency tiers,
- Maps real-time deployment metrics: food delivered, wells dug, systems built,
- Cross-references third-party audits and GPS-verified impact markers.

For example, clicking on Rafael Moreno's 2033 contribution shows:

- $3.6B routed to Dhaka's Urban Food Grid,
- Deployment timeline from procurement to delivery,
- Real-time outcomes (caloric intake, vendor network coverage, job creation).

3. Outcome Channel

- Integrates longitudinal impact data with regional goals and thresholds (e.g., SDG alignment, child mortality reduction),
- Publishes third-party evaluations and crowd-based testimonials,
- Includes a **citizen validation system**, where individuals in recipient zones can confirm

delivery and performance via SMS or encrypted voice transmission.

All three channels are **public, multilingual, decentralized,** and **AI-flagged for anomalies**—with any suspicious activity immediately sent to:

- The **Independent Ethics Tribunal,**
- The **Global Citizen Jury (annually elected),**
- And open-source watchdog forums for review.

Why Radical Visibility Matters
When accountability is visible:

- Corruption fears shrink,
- Public trust expands,
- And the conversation shifts from *"Will they give?"* to *"Are they giving what they owe—and is it working?"*

In a world that has grown cynical about wealth, this visibility is not just a reform—it is **a revolution of confidence.**

It restores the **moral license of power**—not through charisma or PR, but through measurable, audited, visible duty.

Imagine a world where:

- Schoolchildren can pull up their region's water system status on a tablet,
- Farmers can view their local food price stabilization fund's source and expiration date,

- Journalists can compare contribution patterns across all trillionaires on a searchable public dashboard.

That world exists.
It's just a click away.

"Audit by the People" – **The Rise of Participatory Compliance**
Perhaps the most radical feature of the DLS is its **citizen-facing compliance model.**
Any person—anywhere in the world—can:

- File a claim of unmet delivery,
- Upload photos, testimonials, or metadata to validate or contest official impact reports,
- Access plain-language legal summaries of all obligation rules.

Each validated claim becomes part of the **Global Performance Archive**, used by:

- The Public Ethics Council (Chapter 6),
- The Humanity Guarantee Fund Board,
- Policy researchers and reformers.

In other words: *You don't need power to hold power accountable anymore. You need only information—and the system provides it.*
This is not the surveillance state.
It's the **transparency society.**
The Tribunal for Stewardship Violations

Systems without consequences are merely guidelines. Justice without enforcement is only poetry.

That's why the Trillionaire Responsibility Framework does not end with data dashboards and transparency tools —it includes a binding, enforceable, and globally recognized legal mechanism: the **Tribunal for Stewardship Violations (TSV).**

The TSV is not a metaphor. It is a real, treaty-bound court empowered to:

- Investigate,
- Arbitrate,
- Penalize,
- And, if necessary, confiscate contributions owed by any trillionaire failing to meet their obligations under the Global Treaty on Trillionaire Responsibility (GTTRRC).

This part outlines how the tribunal functions, its scope of power, precedent-setting authority, and how it ensures **no trillionaire escapes accountability—regardless of location, status, or corporate structure.**

THE AUTHORITY **of the Tribunal**

The TSV was established under **Article VI of the GTTRRC,** signed by over 160 countries and legally harmonized with:

- The International Criminal Court (ICC),
- The Financial Action Task Force (FATF),
- The International Court of Justice (ICJ),

- And participating jurisdictions' national enforcement arms.

Its power includes:

- **Subpoena of global asset data,**
- **Freezing and redirecting funds** through partner financial institutions,
- **Ruling on stewardship evasion claims,** including underreporting, shell transfers, and synthetic asset shelters,
- **Imposing noncompliance penalties,** from financial surcharges to temporary economic disqualification (TED)—a legal status that suspends elite economic privileges until contribution is fulfilled.

Trillionaires are not above the law.
They are now **accountable to the planet's highest humanitarian court.**

Structure of the Tribunal

The TSV is composed of:

- **Nine permanent judges,** elected by the UN General Assembly from a pool of candidates with expertise in global finance, human rights law, tax enforcement, and ethics.
- **Four rotating citizen arbiters,** drawn annually from signatory nations and trained via the GCFWS judicial program.

- **One Indigenous or stateless representative,** ensuring representation of communities most affected by global inequality and environmental destruction.

Cases are heard **three times annually**, and rulings are:

- Binding,
- Public,
- And precedented—meaning future noncompliant trillionaires can be held accountable based on prior verdicts.

Decisions are published in all UN-recognized languages and accompanied by plain-language summaries available through the Digital Ledger of Stewardship interface.

The Three Tiers of Violation

To ensure proportionality, the Tribunal uses a three-tier system for violations:

Tier 1: Delinquency (Failure to Pay on Time)

- Triggered when a required contribution is **30+ days overdue.**
- Response: Public notification, interest surcharge, and restricted financial privileges (e.g., luxury capital freeze).

Tier 2: Deception (Asset Evasion or Misreporting)

- Triggered when forensic audits

uncover **fraudulent accounting, offshore concealment, or willful underreporting.**
- Response: Full retroactive repayment, penalty up to 300% of original obligation, 2-year TED status, and public listing on the **Stewardship Evasion Register (SER).**

Tier 3: Sabotage (Interference with the GCFWS or DLS)

- Triggered when a trillionaire, their proxy, or affiliated entity attempts to **hack, coerce, or dismantle the responsibility system.**
- Response: Emergency seizure of assets via international banking sanctions, 10-year TED status, and lifetime loss of committee voting privileges.

This tiered system ensures **balance between enforcement and integrity**—punishing bad faith while rewarding compliance and transparency.

A Global Enforcement Web

The TSV does not rely on force. It relies on **systems— already in place.**

Once a ruling is made:

- Banks freeze assets through interbank regulatory compliance.
- Customs authorities halt transfers of property, luxury items, and financial instruments.

- Trade partners can deny privileged contracts to noncompliant entities.
- Travel is restricted under **Diplomatic Financial Noncompliance Protocol (DFNP)**—akin to a fiscal passport freeze.

In other words:
You can run, but your money can't.

LEGAL PRECEDENT: Case #003 – The Gibraltar Holdings Ruling

In 2031, the Tribunal heard its third case: **The People vs. Gibraltar Holdings,** a shell conglomerate traced to a trillionaire who attempted to:

- Obscure $2.7 billion in tokenized real estate assets,
- Reclassify public-private infrastructure bonds as "philanthropy,"
- And delay water relief funding in the Sahel by six months.

Outcome:

- **Full restitution ordered,**
- $8.2 billion penalty for economic sabotage,
- Lifetime TED status applied,
- Chairmanship rights on two GCFWS subcommittees revoked.

Public trust in the system soared.

And global compliance rates improved by 22% the following year.

This wasn't just punishment.

It was **justice with teeth.**

The Age of Unenforced Power Is Over

With the Tribunal in place:

- Every contribution is real,
- Every delay is monitored,
- Every bad actor is known.

This isn't the end of financial power—it's the **democratization of enforcement.**

It means the richest humans in history are **finally part of a system they cannot control—only serve.**

And in that, the world gains something it never had before:

A law that protects the many from the indifference of the few.

The Global Citizen Jury – A New Model of People-Powered Oversight

For centuries, the global public has been told to wait.

Wait for justice.

Wait for reform.

Wait for the powerful to listen.

No longer.

The **Global Citizen Jury (GCJ)** is one of the most radical innovations of the Trillionaire Responsibility Framework—a mechanism that ensures the **world's richest individuals are evaluated not only by experts or economists, but by the people their power touches most.**

This part of the chapter explores how the GCJ works, how it amplifies moral authority from the ground up, and how it puts **ordinary people in extraordinary positions of oversight.**

WHY THE GCJ Exists

Transparency and enforcement are essential. But alone, they risk becoming technocratic—systems of data and law that remain detached from lived experience. The GCJ was created to bridge that gap, allowing for:

- **Democratic legitimacy:** Wealth affects everyone; so everyone deserves a voice in evaluating how it is wielded.
- **Cultural accountability:** Metrics don't always reflect dignity, respect, or the nuances of local impact.
- **Moral check:** Billionaires can hire consultants. Trillionaires can hire compliance officers. But they cannot buy the approval of ordinary people.

In short: the GCJ is where the **heart meets the ledger.**

HOW THE JURY Is Formed

Each year, 54 citizens—**one from every signatory country**—are randomly selected using a double-blind algorithm that ensures:

- **Demographic balance** across age, gender, economic status, and education,

- **Geographic diversity,** with rotating urban, rural, and Indigenous representation,
- **Exclusion of elite affiliations,** including wealth over a threshold or high-ranking political status.

All members undergo a one-month **orientation and ethics immersion,** delivered in their native languages, covering:

- The structure of the GCFWS and HGF,
- The Digital Ledger of Stewardship,
- And principles of humanitarian accountability.

They serve one **non-renewable, one-year term.**
Participation is compensated, protected by law, and—where needed—confidential.

What the Jury Does
The Global Citizen Jury produces two primary outputs:
1. **The Annual Stewardship Review**

- A 200-page public report that:
    - Scores each trillionaire's performance across transparency, timeliness, ethical behavior, and transformative impact;
    - Highlights gaps between funding and lived outcomes (including emotional, cultural, and dignity-based metrics);
    - Includes field interviews, photojournalism, and short testimonials from impacted communities.

Scores are color-coded:

- **Green:** Aligned with spirit and letter of obligation
- **Yellow:** Procedurally compliant but morally questionable
- **Red:** Failing public expectation, even if legally compliant

These ratings don't replace the Tribunal—but they **shape public perception and policy reform.** Many trillionaires respond directly in public forums to their GCJ ratings.

2. Emergency Hearings

If a whistleblower report or mass citizen claim is filed against a committee member, the GCJ can:

- Convene a public virtual hearing (translated in 30+ languages),
- Review testimony and evidence in real time,
- Vote on whether to refer the case to the **Tribunal for Stewardship Violations,**
- Issue public "calls to redress," which carry major reputational and diplomatic pressure.

The GCJ is **not symbolic.**
Its words move markets.
Its decisions shape discourse.
It is the *conscience of the system.*

EXAMPLES OF IMPACT

The 2032 Orange Score Controversy

When a trillionaire-funded irrigation project in India underdelivered despite full financial compliance, the GCJ investigated. They discovered:

- Funds had been allocated efficiently—but the design lacked local gender inclusion, resulting in women being excluded from co-op benefits.

The jury scored the project "Yellow – Technically Efficient, Socially Harmful," and demanded:

- A new gender equity plan,
- Reallocation of maintenance contracts,
- Public apology by the contributor.

Within months, the program was revised—and **the number of women in co-op leadership tripled.**
The Praise Case – Green Across All Metrics
In 2033, the jury unanimously issued a **Green rating with Commendation** to a trillionaire whose water sanitation rollout in Central Africa included:

- Decentralized local ownership,
- Cultural rituals incorporated in design,
- And open employment of former refugees.

That contributor's reputation soared—not due to branding, but due to **earned moral legitimacy.**

When the World **Watches Together**
The Global Citizen Jury hearings are among the **most-watched broadcasts on Earth**—translated in 60+

languages, replayed in schools, streamed on open-access platforms, and discussed across social media.
Because people are not just observers.
They are **participants in power.**
And that power comes not from wealth or weaponry, but from truth-telling at scale.
In this system, no one is too rich to be rated.
No one is too powerful to be asked: *"Are you doing what you owe?"*
And **for the first time in history**, the people who used to wait for justice—**are now delivering it.**
Public Trust and the New Transparency Economy
If Chapter 9 began by asking *how do we enforce responsibility across borders?*, it ends with a deeper question:
What happens to a society when trust is no longer the exception—but the system itself?
The final component of global accountability is not technological. It's **cultural.** It is the architecture of **public trust**—not built on blind faith, nor manufactured credibility, but on systems so visible, so fair, and so reciprocal that **citizens begin to believe again.**
This part explores how the Trillionaire Responsibility Framework and its transparency tools are creating an **entirely new economy of trust**—where legitimacy is earned, not inherited, and where power flows **toward responsibility**, not away from it.

BEYOND COMPLIANCE: **The Rise of Voluntary Overdelivery**
In the first five years of the Humanity Guarantee Fund's operation, enforcement tools were essential. But by the second wave of trillionaires (2030–2035), a cultural shift began to emerge:

- Trillionaires began **competing not on wealth alone, but on stewardship scores.**
- Contributors who exceeded their mandated obligations were publicly praised—not through awards, but by **citizen narratives** shared globally.
- Those who earned multiple "Green with Commendation" ratings from the Global Citizen Jury began influencing others—not through intimidation, but through **moral leadership.**

This phenomenon is now known as **Voluntary Overdelivery (VOD)**—the act of contributing **more than the legal minimum** not for tax breaks or headlines, but because **the new status symbol is stewardship.**

Reputation in this new era isn't built on yachts, space flights, or stadiums.

It's built on:

- Impact dashboards glowing green,
- Citizen testimonials from across the globe,
- And trust—not just in what you say, but in what the world can verify.

The Transparency Economy

The digital era commodified data. The surveillance era commodified people. But in the **transparency economy**, legitimacy is the most valuable currency—and it can't be purchased. It must be **performed, proven, and preserved.**

Within this ecosystem:

- NGOs and watchdog groups **partner with the DLS** to build publicly accessible scorecards.
- Journalists use **impact verification algorithms** to cross-reference claims with outcomes.
- Universities and think tanks track **civic compliance indexes,** rating not just corporations —but individuals—on equity, climate impact, and stewardship duty.

Trillionaires now build *"Trust Teams"*—advisors, ethicists, and public dialogue staff—tasked with maintaining alignment between contribution, impact, and citizen expectation.

And markets are responding:

- Cities and countries prioritize contracts with "Certified Steward" contributors.
- Foundations refuse partnerships with red-listed funders.
- Consumers are now more likely to purchase from brands **with visible links to GCFWS-aligned responsibility.**

Trust has become a measurable asset class.

THE DECLINE **of Performative Philanthropy**
Gone are the days of:

- Donor walls,
- Naming rights,
- Legacy foundations shielded by bureaucracy.

In the transparency economy, what matters is:

- Did the money arrive?
- Did it help?
- Do the people it was meant for confirm that it worked?

The Global Citizen Jury has ended the age of selective storytelling.

The Digital Ledger of Stewardship has ended the age of hidden evasion.

And the Tribunal has ended the age of impunity.

Now, even well-intentioned philanthropists must ask themselves: *Is this just generous—or is it just?*

What This Means for the World

We've entered a new ethical phase in global civilization:

- **Where wealth is not hidden, but harnessed.**
- **Where power is not admired, but audited.**
- **Where contribution is not optional, but expected.**

And most importantly:

Where trust is no longer a public illusion—it is a public record.

This doesn't mean perfection.

But it means **permanence of purpose.**

It means:

- Every child can look up where their water came from.

- Every citizen can ask who built the system they rely on—and see the truth.
- Every trillionaire can no longer pretend their power is neutral.

Because now, the world can see everything.
And with that vision comes **not fear—but faith, earned in public.**

10

A NEW SOCIAL CONTRACT

Redefining the Role of the Ultra-Wealthy
The phrase *"social contract"* was once a revolutionary idea.

Rousseau, Locke, Hobbes—each envisioned a society where **individual freedom was balanced with collective responsibility.**

Governments gained legitimacy by serving the public good. Citizens obeyed the law because the law protected life, liberty, and livelihood.

But here, in the 21st century, **the old contract is broken.**

Not by the poor. Not by the middle class.

But by those whose wealth now exceeds that of entire nations—who benefit from global systems, yet answer to none.

It is time to forge a **new contract**—one that addresses the rise of **sovereign individuals** with trillion-dollar reach and responsibilities.

This part defines what that contract looks like: morally, economically, and structurally.

. . .

The Collapse of the Old Contract

The traditional social contract relied on nation-states to:

- Collect taxes,
- Enforce laws,
- Provide public services,
- Regulate behavior in exchange for civil protection.

But the global economy has outgrown this model. Today:

- Trillionaires operate across borders, while laws stop at borders.
- Mega-corporations pay less tax than schoolteachers.
- Philanthropy replaces governance in health, food, and education.

In this vacuum:

- **Trust decays,**
- **Institutions hollow,**
- **Civic morale collapses.**

The social contract frays—not because people expect too much, but because **those with the most give the least, and suffer no consequences for it.**

The Moral Case for a New Role

Extreme wealth in the 21st century carries with it more than financial power—it carries:

- Environmental consequence,
- Social consequence,
- Political consequence,
- Cultural consequence.

The ultra-wealthy don't just influence markets. They influence **narratives, norms, and national priorities.**

That's why the new social contract demands **a new archetype of leadership:**

- Not the genius CEO.
- Not the benevolent philanthropist.
- Not the distant investor.

But the **planetary steward**—an individual whose wealth automatically binds them to the **well-being of humanity and the biosphere.**

In this paradigm:

- Responsibility is not reputational. It is *relational*.
- Ownership is not sovereignty. It is *trusteeship*.
- Power is not a prize. It is *a service platform for survival*.

DEFINING **the Trillionaire's Civic Identity**

What does it mean to be a trillionaire in a world of famine and floods?

It means your financial footprint equals that of entire continents.

It means your decisions—on investment, on timing, on speech—can accelerate or prevent:

- Climate migration,
- Resource wars,
- Food shortages,
- And generational trauma.

Thus, the trillionaire is no longer a private citizen. They are a **public actor by scale**, even if not by choice. The new social contract redefines their identity as:

- **Automatically enrolled** in the systems that govern humanity's future,
- **Permanently responsible** for impact proportional to capacity,
- **Structurally obligated** to serve—not control—the collective good.

They may still innovate. They may still own. They may still build empires.

But **they cannot opt out.**

Because freedom at the trillion-dollar level, without obligation, is not liberty—it is lawlessness in disguise.

From Privilege to **Public Utility**

This transformation is not punitive.

It is **protective.** It protects:

- The legitimacy of capitalism,
- The stability of markets,
- The moral fabric of society.

Without this transformation, capitalism becomes

feudalism—where privilege consolidates and systems rot beneath inequality.

But with a binding role for the ultra-wealthy, we create a world where:

- Innovation funds eradication of hunger,
- Wealth builds instead of withholds,
- And the richest become not untouchable— but **unignorably responsible.**

This is the new contract.

And it begins not with negotiation—but with **non-negotiable duty.**

The Rights of the Vulnerable – Making Survival Non-Negotiable

A social contract is only as strong as the protection it offers the weakest.

It cannot be measured by the liberty of the powerful— but by the **dignity, safety, and freedom of those most at risk.**

In the 20th century, the language of rights grew more expansive:

- Civil rights, political rights, women's rights, LGBTQ+ rights.
- The right to vote, to speak, to be safe from violence.

But in the 21st century, a more urgent question has emerged:

What good is a voice if your stomach is empty? What good is liberty without water?

This part of the chapter reframes the foundation of the

new social contract as a **Rights-Based Mandate for Human Survival**—not as charity, not as aid, but as **non-negotiable entitlements** enforceable through the global obligation of the ultra-wealthy.

Survival **as the First Right**

Before speech, before property, before protest—comes breath.

There is no freedom without food.

No justice without clean water.

No peace where famine prevails.

Thus, the first right of the vulnerable in the new social contract is this:

The right to life-supporting infrastructure, guaranteed by those whose wealth surpasses the scale of government.

In practice, this means:

- Food access is not subject to geopolitics or donor fatigue.
- Water access is not stalled by logistics or ignored by investors.
- Nutrition, hydration, and sanitation are no longer **favors from the powerful,** but **claims of the people.**

This right is not rhetorical. It is **institutionalized in the Humanity Guarantee Fund and enforced by global law.**

Shifting **From Aid to Entitlement**

Historically, aid systems were designed as:

- Reactive,
- Politicized,
- And often based on **who mattered to whom.**

That meant:

- Certain crises received attention, others didn't.
- Certain faces unlocked empathy, others were ignored.
- Certain tragedies were declared emergencies; others were rendered statistics.

The new social contract flips this paradigm.
In this framework:

- The *vulnerable no longer wait* for the benevolence of the rich.
- Hunger is addressed not with donations, but **debt owed by global capital.**
- The child in Yemen, the grandmother in Somalia, the schoolgirl in Haiti—**are stakeholders**, not afterthoughts.

Their existence activates action.
Their survival is guaranteed not by mercy—but by **mandated fiscal responsibility.**

Legal Rights, **Not Aspirational Goals**
The Sustainable Development Goals (SDGs) called for "zero hunger" and "clean water for all."
But they were **targets**, not **rights.**
The new social contract:

- Embeds those goals in **binding treaty law,**
- Links unmet needs to **enforceable obligations from trillionaire committee members,**
- And allows for **legal recourse when survival systems fail.**

If the Humanity Guarantee Fund fails to deliver access:

- Citizens can file claims.
- Cases can be heard by the Tribunal.
- Penalties can be imposed.
- Funds can be redirected until the gap is closed.

This is not a vision board.
This is **governance by moral infrastructure.**

Restoring **Moral Balance**

The rights of the vulnerable are not limited to material survival.

They also include:

- The **right to dignity**—to receive aid without humiliation.
- The **right to truth**—to access data on who funds, delivers, and delays survival.
- The **right to voice**—to rate the systems that affect their lives, through the Global Citizen Jury and participatory evaluation tools.

These rights form a **moral counterweight** to the gravitational pull of elite wealth.

They say:

- You may earn—but you may not neglect.
- You may own—but you may not obscure.
- You may influence—but you may not disappear behind algorithms.

In this contract, the most vulnerable have **more than rights on paper.**
They have **power in law, in data, and in public opinion.**

When Survival Is Non-Negotiable
We must no longer ask:

- *"Can we help them?"*
- *"Should we intervene?"*

We must now say:

- *"We are required to act."*
- *"We are obligated to deliver."*

Because in this social contract, survival is not a side benefit of progress.
It is the **baseline from which all progress must begin.**
Shared Responsibility Across All Classes – A Civilization-Wide Ethic
A fair society doesn't rely on a single class to bear all burdens.
Yes, the ultra-wealthy must be held to the **highest proportional standard**—but a truly resilient civilization is built on a culture of **shared responsibility** that includes:

- The working poor,

The Trillionaire Club

- The middle classes,
- Government officials,
- Entrepreneurs, and
- Emerging generations.

This part expands the moral architecture of the Trillionaire Responsibility Framework into a **civilization-wide ethic,** showing how *everyone*—not just the trillionaires—has a role to play in fulfilling the new social contract.

Because justice doesn't scale through obligation alone.

It scales through **participation.**

WHY SHARED RESPONSIBILITY Matters

The success of the Humanity Guarantee Fund and the Global Committee for Food and Water Security is rooted in:

- Enforcement,
- Structure,
- Legal authority.

But its **endurance** depends on cultural buy-in.

If citizens view global stewardship as someone else's problem—

If nations believe the fund excuses them from governance—

If middle-class donors pull back because "the rich will handle it"—

Then the system will **fail from spiritual atrophy,** not structural flaw.

This chapter declares:

Shared responsibility does not mean equal burden.

It means **mutual commitment, scaled by capacity.**

A Multilayered Model of Participation

Here's how the new social contract activates shared responsibility across all sectors:

1. **For Everyday Citizens:**

- **Engagement:** Use the Digital Ledger of Stewardship to track projects in your region, report gaps, or submit testimonials.
- **Advocacy:** Mobilize civic pressure when enforcement fails or needs reform.
- **Education:** Teach the values of dignity, equity, and planetary stewardship to children—not as idealism, but as **civic foundation.**

No one is too small to participate in this system. Because every voice expands its legitimacy.

2. **For the Global Middle Class:**

- **Co-invest in parallel systems:** community co-ops, sustainable water infrastructure, educational uplift.
- **Refuse performative consumption** and begin aligning values with spending, employment, and investment.
- **Pressure corporate actors** to align with GCFWS standards—not just through ethics, but through wallet-based voting.

Your tax bracket doesn't exempt you from moral agency.

It multiplies it when paired with access, platform, or stability.

3. For Governments:

- **Align national policies** with the principles of the fund—prioritizing universal services, local infrastructure, and anti-corruption laws.
- **Enforce treaty obligations** and contribute to verification tools and enforcement support.
- **Treat international obligation as reciprocity**, not dependence: if trillionaires are held responsible for global need, so must states be held responsible for domestic equity.

Governments are not replaced by the fund.
They are **reinforced by it.**

4. For Businesses and Nonprofits:

- **Adopt the Stewardship Standards Framework**—a voluntary alignment toolkit for ethical supply chains, data transparency, and humanitarian reinvestment.
- **Host participatory platforms** where employees, customers, and beneficiaries can guide impact strategies in line with the global ethic.
- **Innovate in ways that reduce dependency on crisis response**, and instead strengthen resilience through regenerative, inclusive practices.

REBUILDING TRUST IN INSTITUTIONS—TOGETHER
The failure of global trust didn't begin with the wealthy.

It began with **everyone believing someone else would fix it.**
But now, with a system in place:

- That makes wealth accountable,
- That makes survival a right,
- That publishes every dollar and decision in real time,

—there is no longer space for resignation.
Now, everyone becomes:

- **A steward** in their own capacity,
- **A partner** in enforcement,
- **A carrier** of moral momentum.

This is how we rebuild trust:
Not through idealism, but through action embedded in design.

SHARED **Responsibility ≠ Equal Sacrifice**
It's important to say this clearly:
Not all sacrifices are equal. Nor should they be.
The burden of feeding the world should not fall on a teacher in Nairobi or a nurse in Detroit.
But the *ethic of care* must be shared.
And when systems work, the moral tone they set permeates:

- The language of journalism,
- The policies of local governance,
- The pedagogy of classrooms,

- The aspirations of youth.

When trillionaires are seen **not as distant anomalies**, but as active agents in a world where *everyone is giving what they can*, the culture becomes one of **participation, not protest.**

The Ethic We Grow Together
The new social contract is not only about what the richest give.
It is about what we **all protect.**

- The idea that every person matters.
- The belief that every life deserves water, food, and dignity.
- The commitment that when we build a system this strong, **we all become part of its guardianship.**

Because stewardship is not a financial tier.
It is a **shared identity.**
The End of Indifference – A Moral Civilization Emerges
Indifference has been the defining sin of the modern world.
Not hate. Not cruelty.
But the quiet shrug when someone suffers far away.
The numbing of hearts in the face of numbers too large to hold.
Fifty million hungry.
Two billion without clean water.
Hundreds of millions displaced by storms, by war, by

greed.
And what did the world do?
We scrolled.
We sighed.
We called it *unfortunate*—but *inevitable*.

This final part of Chapter 10 argues that the greatest revolution sparked by the Trillionaire Responsibility Framework is not economic or technological—it is **moral**.

Because once the world sees that the hunger problem *can* be solved...

Once the water gap *is* bridged with structure, funding, and enforcement...

Then **indifference dies**.

And in its place rises something that has been missing for far too long:

Civic love. Global care. Shared moral direction.

When No One Can Say "We Didn't Know"

The most common justification for inaction is ignorance:

- "I didn't realize it was this bad."
- "I thought someone else was helping."
- "I wasn't sure how to make a difference."

But in the world of the Digital Ledger of Stewardship:

- Every project is visible.
- Every delay is tracked.
- Every trillionaire's fulfillment or failure is public record.

There is no plausible deniability left.
No ignorance shield.
No plausible "not my problem."
Now, when someone dies of hunger in a trillionaire's assigned region, the cause is not fate—it is **fiscal failure**.
And that knowledge changes everyone:

- Students begin to ask tougher questions in school.
- Voters demand accountability from governments aligned with red-listed trillionaires.
- Creators and storytellers shape narratives of justice, responsibility, and the **death of apathy**.

DISMANTLING **the Spectator Society**
In the 20th century, we watched injustice on TV.
In the 21st century, we clicked past it.
Now, in this era of shared stewardship, **passivity is no longer morally neutral**.
This is not a surveillance state.
This is a **participatory civilization**.
Where:

- Accountability is a public sport.
- Trustworthiness is the new luxury.
- And moral clarity is not just for philosophers— it's built into dashboards, treaties, and everyday language.

We don't wait for heroes anymore.
We build systems that make **heroism systemic**.

. . .

THE SPIRITUAL SHIFT: From Isolation to Belonging
There's a deeper undercurrent to all of this.
When people know:

- That someone will have clean water because a trillionaire fulfilled their duty,
- That a war-torn region is eating again because justice was funded—not debated,
- That survival is no longer optional, but expected—

They begin to feel something we lost for decades:
We are part of something that works.
This is the spiritual function of the new social contract.
Not just to regulate. But to **restore belonging.**
Not just to mandate. But to **reinvigorate meaning.**
A moral civilization is one where:

- No wealth is without responsibility,
- No life is without value,
- And no person, no matter how distant, is **beyond our moral horizon.**

WHAT COMES AFTER INDIFFERENCE?
After indifference comes movement.

- The movement of resources where they're most needed.
- The movement of values from theory into law.

- The movement of a people—not toward survival alone, but toward **shared stewardship of the world itself.**

The old story said: "That's not our problem."
The new story says: "If it touches any of us, it belongs to all of us."
That is the end of indifference.
And the birth of **a moral civilization.**

11

A TRILLIONAIRE DIES HUNGRY
THE PARABLE OF KELLAN RYSE

"He built a fortress of wealth so high, he forgot there was no door."
— Inscription found on the wall of the Ryse Estate, 2045

This chapter begins with a parable. It's fictional—but entirely plausible.

Kellan Ryse was the first person in recorded history to achieve a verified **net worth of $3 trillion.** He was a visionary technologist, a master of vertical integration, and the architect of a quantum data empire that underpinned nearly every global transaction by 2036.

He was also the **first person to die from voluntary starvation while holding more capital than 86 nations combined.**

His story is not a tragedy of miscalculation.

It is a tragedy of **moral design failure.**

It is a warning about what happens when freedom is disconnected from obligation—and when wealth becomes so concentrated it ceases to recognize the world around it.

This fictional narrative is presented as a moral fable for our time.

The Fortress

By 2038, Ryse had withdrawn from most public appearances. He lived inside **an autonomous, AI-managed compound** spanning seven miles of protected tundra in Northern Canada. The compound had:

- Food labs,
- Vertical farms,
- Medical AI assistants,
- And private satellites to ensure uninterrupted communications.

He claimed he was **"independent of global systems."**

But when the Great Dust Years hit—a convergence of climate crop failures, antibiotic resistance, and economic unrest—supply chains buckled in ways even quantum forecasting failed to predict.

One day, a fungal contamination spread through his compound's food production units.

The backup reserve of protein compounds had expired.

And no outside assistance came.

Why?

Because Kellan Ryse had **opted out** of the Global Committee for Food and Water Security.

He had rejected the Trillionaire Responsibility Framework.

He lobbied against the Global Treaty on Trillionaire Responsibility.

He believed: "I can take care of myself."

Until he couldn't.

The Collapse of Autonomy

When his AI systems flagged food shortages, they requested emergency resupply under the GCFWS Emergency Activation Protocol. But the tribunal returned a simple statement:

"Mr. Ryse is in breach of mandatory stewardship obligations. He is listed as noncompliant. Until restitution is made, emergency services are unavailable."

Even then, Ryse had options. He could:

- Release $1 billion into the fund.
- Acknowledge legal obligation.
- Join the system he had scorned.

Instead, he refused.

He called it **"extortion through humanitarian guilt."**

By the third month, he was subsisting on filtered rainwater and the remnants of nutrition gel from a corporate archive.

By the fifth, he stopped appearing on his satellite feed.

His final message, intercepted by a public access channel, read:

"I owned everything. But I was never part of anything."

"I believed in systems until they needed me to share."

The Lessons of Ryse

Though fictional, the story of Kellan Ryse captures a chilling truth:

Without participation, wealth is isolation.

**Without stewardship, power becomes irrelevant.
Without obligation, no one—not even a trillionaire—
is safe.**
This parable teaches that:

- Autonomy is a myth at scale.
- The richest cannot self-sustain through architecture alone.
- The world no longer allows hoarding without consequence.

Kellan Ryse's death was not from hunger.
It was from **philosophical starvation.**
He refused to belong—and the world let him live out his fantasy.
Until nature made the final call.

The Heir Who Returned the Fortune

In a world dominated by legacy, few question inheritance.
But this parable tells the story of someone who did.

Alina Voss was 32 when she inherited **$1.7 trillion**—a synthetic wealth portfolio stretching across offshore quantum assets, carbon markets, orbital satellite infrastructure, and neurotech patents from her father, Ronan Voss.

Her father had been a libertarian capitalist of the old world—a man who believed **freedom was defined by detachment**, and that "the only public good is private innovation." He refused to join the Global Committee. He died during the **Sri Lanka Blackout,** when his private hospital's AI systems were denied firmware updates under Global Compliance Policy.

Alina watched him die through a bulletproof glass panel

—separated from the ventilator he helped design but could no longer access.

He left her everything.

The Decision

She sat with the inheritance for 33 days. No press releases. No transactions. Just silence. Her advisors urged her to:

- Activate privacy accounts,
- Convert her assets to decentralized protocols,
- Liquidate and escape regulation.

But she had grown up watching the world fracture under wealth hoarding.

She had seen children wash blood from water barrels.

She had taken unsanctioned university classes in **post-capitalist ethics**.

So she logged into the Humanity Guarantee Fund portal.

And she typed a single sentence:

"I hereby surrender 92% of this fortune to the global commons. I request enrollment, not exemption."

It shocked the world.

It disarmed the skeptics.

It *broke the algorithm.*

The Transformation

Alina Voss didn't disappear. She **participated**.

- She became Chair of the Global Committee for Food and Water Security by age 35.
- She built **the first transgenerational stewardship school**—training heirs in ethics, equity, and ecological responsibility before they ever touched a dollar.
- She issued **the Moral Wealth Manifesto**, co-signed by 17 trillionaire successors in the next decade.

Her leadership was quiet. Humble. Measured.
She didn't build rockets. She built **root systems**.
The people she fed will never know her face.
The children who drink because of her won't remember her name.
But every steward since has cited **The Voss Pivot** as the moment history **turned toward moral capital.**

THE LEGACY **She Chose**

By age 50, Alina's net worth had dropped to $36 million —still comfortable, but no longer structural.

She lived in a **shared regenerative village in Patagonia**, where her responsibilities included:

- Hosting water conflict mediation sessions,
- Planting biointensive gardens,
- And mentoring teenage climate activists on resource law.

When asked once on a global panel, "Why did you give it all away?" she responded:

"I didn't give it away. I gave it back. Wealth is not ownership. It is custody. And I was tired of holding what wasn't mine."

MORAL OF THE **Parable**

If Kellan Ryse teaches us what happens when wealth detaches,

Alina Voss shows what happens when wealth reconnects.

She reminds us:

- That **legacy is not accumulation**—it is contribution.
- That **leadership is not control**—it is custodianship.
- That **wealth does not define you**—but how you return it might.

In a world once ruled by hoarding, she redefined prosperity as **participation in collective well-being.**
And for that, she became not a trillionaire—
But a symbol of **the civilization we could become.**
The Committee's Hardest Vote
Every system, no matter how noble, will face a test.
A moment when ideals collide with reality.
When the letter of the law clashes with the beating heart of its purpose.
This is the story of that moment—when the **Global Committee for Food and Water Security (GCFWS)** faced its most morally complex decision.
Not about money.
Not about policy.

But about **life, limits, and the meaning of responsibility.**

The Emergency

In the year 2042, the world experienced the **Great Inland Drought**—a once-in-a-century hydrological event that turned the rivers of Central Asia into cracked silence.

- 27 million people were without drinking water across Kazakhstan, Uzbekistan, and western China.
- Food systems collapsed.
- Infants died of dehydration in refugee camps ringed by sand.

The GCFWS, through the Humanity Guarantee Fund, had already allocated its full emergency budget for the year: $405 billion had been deployed across three continents.
But this was different.
This drought had no precedent.
It demanded an additional $43 billion within 21 days—
Or entire populations would be lost.
The emergency subcommittee presented the options to the full Global Committee:

- Delay other projects to reallocate funds.
- Trigger a once-in-a-decade override of stewardship protocols, enforcing additional emergency contributions from all active trillionaire members.

The override had **never been used.**

It would break protocol.
It would force contributions beyond annual obligations.
It would **test the very boundaries of voluntary overdelivery.**

The Debate

The Committee convened for 36 hours without pause.
Arguments were intense. Measured. Emotional.
For the override:

- "What good is protocol if it costs 4,000 lives a day?"
- "This is why the Fund exists—to flex when the world breaks."
- "We have built accountability. Now we must test compassion."

Against the override:

- "It sets a precedent that destabilizes predictable stewardship."
- "Some contributors will flee the system. Trust may fracture."
- "We are asking for more than money—we are demanding surrender."

But then, a voice cut through the noise.
It was **Einar Njord**, a reluctant committee member who had never spoken during a plenary.
His net worth: $1.1 trillion.
His tone: steady, quiet, weathered.
"I joined this committee because I was forced to.

Today I vote for the override because I choose to.
Because if we cannot act now, we are not a committee.
We are an accounting firm with delusions of conscience."
Silence followed.
Then the vote was called.

The Decision

The override passed: 37–5, with 4 abstentions.
Within 12 hours:

- The emergency funds were released.
- New desalination systems were flown to the Aral Basin.
- Mobile filtration tanks were dropped via vertical air columns into Uzbekistan.
- Infants began receiving clean IVs in desert tents that had known only dust.

Four months later, mortality across the drought zone had dropped by 92%.
The override was never needed again.
But it became a **foundational story**—retold in law schools, leadership courses, and village councils alike.
It proved the committee was not just lawful.
It was **moral**.

Why It Mattered

Every system must face its trial.
The moment when:

- Contracts are tested by conscience.
- Leadership requires risk.
- The line between obligation and opportunity vanishes.

The Committee's hardest vote revealed the truth behind all great systems:

The most powerful rules are the ones we break—when the breaking saves lives.

And it left the world with a blueprint for what responsible wealth can become when power is paired with courage.

The Girl Who Read the Ledger

Her name was Amara. She was twelve.

She lived in a tent made of stitched tarpaulin and solar cloth, on the southern edge of what was once the Tigris River.

Her world was heat, hunger, and long walks for water.

Her mother taught her math with rocks. Her father taught her silence.

One morning, a volunteer teacher arrived from the GCFWS Field Access Program. She carried nothing but a tablet.

The lesson was not math.

It was not history.

It was **how to read the Digital Ledger of Stewardship.**

THE FIRST LESSON: **Names and Numbers**

Amara stared at the tablet's screen—struggling to understand why someone had **$2.4 trillion**, while others had nothing.

But then the teacher showed her something else:

- The green badge next to a contributor's name.
- The allocation map showing funds flowing to northern Iraq.
- The list of solar well systems deployed just 200 kilometers north.
- The line that read: *"Funded by the Humanity Guarantee Fund – Verified 3.2M beneficiaries."*

Amara raised her hand and asked:
"So this person helped feed us?"
The teacher nodded.
Amara looked back at the screen.
She traced her finger over the name: **Sebastian Ko.**
"Who is he?" she asked.
"A trillionaire," the teacher replied.
"What's that?"
"Someone very rich," the teacher said.
"But not just rich," Amara said.
"Someone who **helps when they're supposed to.**"

THE LEDGER BECOMES Language

Over the next year, Amara read the Ledger every day. She would:

- Check the water project status like other kids checked the weather.
- Send SMS ratings to confirm whether her local well was working.
- Compare contributors by region: "The woman from Norway is faster than the man from Texas."

Soon, her schoolmates joined her.

By age 13, Amara was presenting GCFWS deployment data to her village council—explaining how many kiloliters had been delivered that quarter, and which contributors were late on their disbursements.

"The system works," she told them, "because we **watch it.**"

THE SHIFT

What happened to Amara wasn't an exception. It was **the system working as intended:**

- When transparency is real,
- When stewardship is verifiable,
- When data meets dignity,

—**knowledge becomes power for those who once had none.**

Because the Ledger is not just a spreadsheet.
It is a **mirror of moral participation.**
And Amara?
She saw herself in it.

YEARS **Later**

Amara grew up.
She became a water engineer.
Then a regional GCFWS planner.
Then a contributor—not in billions, but in blueprints.
At age 29, she stood before the Global Committee.
Not as a steward. Not as a beneficiary.
But as the first person raised **inside the system of planetary responsibility.**

She carried with her the same tablet.
The same questions.
And she said:
"I used to read the Ledger to survive.
Now I help write it—so no one has to wonder who cares anymore."

THE MORAL
This final fictional future is not about wealth.
It is about **belonging**.
Amara's life is what happens when:

- Systems are just,
- Visibility is shared,
- And stewardship becomes part of a child's vocabulary.

She is not saved by the system.
She **joins it. Shapes it. Proves it.**
Because the greatest legacy of the Trillionaire Responsibility Framework is not the money it moved—
But the minds it awakened.

12

FROM BOOK TO BLUEPRINT
FROM CONCEPT TO COALITION – THE PATH TO A GLOBAL TREATY

The Trillionaire Responsibility Framework is not a utopian dream.

It is a **workable, enforceable, and timely proposal**—ready to enter the world through policy, diplomacy, and public pressure.

This part walks through the real-world steps for turning the ideas in this book into a **binding international treaty**—one that can **transform wealth from private luxury into planetary security.**

STEP ONE: **Public Legitimacy Through Moral Clarity**
No treaty can succeed without **popular legitimacy.**
The first step is not legal—it is **narrative.**
This book becomes the seed of that narrative. From here, we build:

- **Public awareness campaigns** that frame the issue of trillionaire responsibility in moral terms: *"The power to end hunger is here. Why isn't it*

The Trillionaire Club

being used?"

- **Digital storytelling efforts** using real data visualizations of existing wealth, cost of solutions, and the mechanics of the Humanity Guarantee Fund.
- **Global media partnerships** to feature investigative journalism, documentaries, and opinion leadership around the premise: *"Wealth that doesn't serve life is waste."*

The goal:
Make the framework so **morally self-evident** that even trillionaires want to support it—or fear public backlash if they don't.

STEP TWO: **Policy Incubation via Global Governance Institutions**

The second step is to introduce the framework to the international policymaking ecosystem.

This begins by:

- Presenting the core ideas to **UN General Assembly Special Sessions**, particularly under Sustainable Development Goals 1 (No Poverty), 2 (Zero Hunger), and 6 (Clean Water).
- Building coalitions among **middle-income nations**, which have the most to gain from equitable funding flows.
- Launching **pilot programs**, funded by voluntary contributors and tracked in real time, to demonstrate proof of concept (e.g., regional food

sovereignty projects or water infrastructure overseen by citizen panels).

In parallel, the framework is integrated into:

- **World Bank and IMF debt negotiations,** encouraging debt restructuring tied to GCFWS alignment.
- **OECD working groups,** particularly those focused on digital wealth taxation and transnational capital mobility.

The key is **momentum from the middle out**—not waiting for G7 approval, but building pressure from multilateral institutions and frontline nations.

STEP THREE: **Drafting the Treaty**

Once enough global attention and coalition support is gathered, a treaty is drafted:

- **The Global Treaty on Trillionaire Responsibility and Resource Contribution (GTTRRC)**—as introduced in Chapter 6.
- Drafted in partnership with legal experts from international humanitarian law, finance regulation, and climate governance.
- Includes technical implementation annexes: stewardship enforcement mechanisms, ethics tribunal procedures, digital ledger interoperability, and fund governance.

Treaty features:

- **Trigger clause:** automatic committee enrollment upon reaching verified $1T net worth.
- **Noncompliance penalty structure:** modeled after tax avoidance treaties and WTO enforcement standards.
- **Public transparency mandates:** access to real-time ledgers and citizen participation portals.

The treaty is submitted through:

- **United Nations Treaty Series,**
- **Special session convened under the Economic and Social Council (ECOSOC),**
- Or by a **coalition of at least 40 signatory nations** initiating it under Article 108 of the UN Charter.

STEP FOUR: Enabling Enforcement Infrastructure
No treaty is effective without teeth.
That's why we simultaneously:

- Build out the **Tribunal for Stewardship Violations** (see Chapter 9) through existing international legal forums.
- Establish the **Digital Ledger of Stewardship** as a parallel trust verification network—independent, multilingual, and hosted through federated servers governed by citizen panels and data ethics councils.
- Create treaty-aligned policies at national levels that:

- Recognize the tribunal's judgments,
- Freeze assets under international stewardship delinquency rulings,
- And deny market privileges to red-listed individuals or firms.

This isn't a dream.

It's **legal choreography**—carefully designed to plug into systems that already exist.

WE'VE DONE This Before

Global minimum tax frameworks.
The International Criminal Court.
The Montreal Protocol.
The Paris Agreement.

The world has proven it can act together when the danger is visible.

This time, the danger is silent:

- It's hunger that doesn't make headlines.
- It's thirst in places no one films.
- It's the corrosive power of indifference.

But we now have a **story**, a **structure**, and a **path**.

The book you are reading is step one.

Building the Humanity Guarantee Fund in the Real World

So far, the Humanity Guarantee Fund has been a conceptual institution—designed to channel enforced contributions from trillionaires into hunger elimination and universal water access.

Now we shift from idea to **infrastructure**.

The Trillionaire Club

This section outlines the practical roadmap to **build the Fund in real-world stages**, using existing institutions, technologies, and frameworks—**starting now**, before the first official trillionaire is even enrolled.

Because we do not have to wait to build the mechanism.

We can—and must—build it **before the need becomes catastrophic.**

PHASE ONE: Create the Institutional Seed

Before the full Humanity Guarantee Fund is treaty-bound, we begin with a **pre-institutional prototype**—a legally registered, internationally monitored fund operating on principles of:

- **Transparency** (blockchain-backed ledgers),
- **Proportional obligation** (scaled contributions by wealth class),
- **Need-based allocation** (based on existing UN hunger and water crisis data).

This seed fund would be:

- Hosted by a coalition of **middle-income nations**, emerging economies, and global south leaders,
- Governed by a **Founding Council** of ethicists, economists, humanitarian leaders, and civil society representatives,
- Supported by an **Advisory Council of philanthropists and investors** who agree to voluntarily model what trillionaire stewardship would look like in practice.

This phase proves:

- The tech works.
- The governance model is scalable.
- And impact can be tracked with a real-world user interface.

PHASE TWO: **Build the Public Ledger Infrastructure**

The most critical component of the Fund is **public trust**, and public trust requires **verifiable data**.

So while financial contributions scale slowly, we immediately deploy the **Digital Ledger of Stewardship** (see Chapter 9) in beta form.

- It tracks voluntary contributions at scale (even from billionaires, governments, and ethical corporations).
- It uses **blockchain-based smart contracts** to verify funds received, programs launched, and lives impacted.
- It includes a **citizen validation interface**, allowing SMS and offline regions to report on deployment success or gaps.

Even without the legal requirement for trillionaire contributions, the Ledger creates:

- **Moral pressure,**
- **Cultural expectation,**
- And a new **benchmark for legitimacy** among global elites.

Think of it as **Glassdoor for global responsibility**—but enforced by public data, not anonymous reviews.

PHASE THREE: **Run Regional Demonstration Projects**

We select **3–5 high-need, high-impact regions** to serve as proof-of-concept deployment sites for the Fund's impact model.

These may include:

- Clean water rollouts in the Sahel,
- Urban food stability systems in South Asia,
- Drought-resistant agricultural co-ops in Central America.

Each project is:

- **Fully traceable** on the Digital Ledger,
- **Co-governed** by local councils, community leaders, and GCFWS representatives,
- And **independently audited** by international universities and public agencies.

These demonstration projects:

- Provide living evidence that the Fund can deliver without waste,
- Serve as **onboarding experiences for future contributors**,
- And create a global body of **data and testimony** to support treaty ratification.

PHASE FOUR: **Align with Global Financial Systems**
Simultaneously, we work to align the Humanity Guarantee Fund with:

- **International Monetary Fund protocols** on capital movement and digital asset tracking,
- **G20 and OECD agreements** on minimum corporate taxation and fiscal transparency,
- **World Bank and regional development bank infrastructure**, leveraging their institutional reach while elevating humanitarian accountability.

By integrating the Fund with **real-time financial clearinghouses**, we create mechanisms where:

- Stewardship payments are **automatically calculated and collected** when thresholds are met,
- Digital assets and offshore accounts can no longer be used to dodge responsibility,
- And **asset verification becomes global, not national.**

The goal:
Make evasion impossible. Make participation seamless.

PHASE FIVE: **Transition to Treaty-Enforced Status**
Once these pillars are in place—legitimacy, tech, proof, alignment—we initiate the **transition to treaty-backed enforcement** (see Part I).

This includes:

- Elevating the Fund's governance body to treaty-recognized legal status,
- Transferring voluntary contributors into **automatic stewardship enrollees** as their wealth crosses treaty-defined thresholds,
- Launching the **Global Tribunal and Public Ethics Oversight Boards**, codifying long-term enforcement and citizen participation.

At this stage, the Humanity Guarantee Fund is **no longer an experiment.**
It is **a permanent institution of global survival.**

What It Will Take

This buildout requires:

- **Visionary funders** to model early adoption,
- **Technologists** to build the ledger infrastructure and accountability tools,
- **Policy architects** to align national and international law,
- **Artists, writers, and educators** to spread the vision into public culture.

It will also require:

- Patience.
- Coalitions.
- And an unshakable moral commitment to the

idea that **hunger and thirst are solvable problems—if we build the right tools.**

And now, the tool has a name:
The Humanity Guarantee Fund.
Strategic Messaging and Public Will – Creating a Cultural Movement
Big systems don't change because of white papers.
They change when **public imagination catches fire.**
When people stop asking, *"Is it realistic?"* and start saying, *"Why hasn't this happened yet?"*

This part shows how to build that fire—by turning the Humanity Guarantee Fund and the Trillionaire Responsibility Framework into a **global cultural movement** through messaging, storytelling, and **strategic moral communication.**

Because behind every successful policy change in modern history—civil rights, global climate accords, marriage equality, truth and reconciliation—there was always a **narrative that shifted culture first.**

THE MESSAGE MUST BE MORAL, Not Technical
Policy speaks in terms of:

- GDP,
- Contribution formulas,
- Cross-border asset verification.

People listen in terms of:

- **Right and wrong,**
- **Life and death,**

- Us and them.

Therefore, our messaging begins with **ethical clarity**:
"If one person can feed a nation, they must.
If one person holds enough to end hunger, and doesn't —they are part of the problem."
That message cannot be abstract. It must be:

- **Sharable** in a sentence,
- **Visualized** with real-world data (e.g., cost of universal water access vs. personal net worth),
- **Rooted in recognizable values**: fairness, stewardship, justice, legacy.

This is not about politics.
It's about the oldest human story:
Will the powerful protect the vulnerable—or pretend they cannot see them?

BUILDING the Narrative Infrastructure
To shift culture, we embed the vision in every form of expression:
1. Media and Journalism

- Partner with investigative outlets to track real-time inequality vs. capacity.
- Launch public dashboards that allow users to explore where billionaires could make the biggest impact.
- Use documentaries, short films, and interviews to humanize the system—and the stakes.

2. Education

- Integrate "planetary stewardship" into civic and ethics curriculums worldwide.
- Launch classroom tools that let students explore the Humanity Guarantee Fund ledger in real time.
- Promote student-led stewardship audits of companies and public figures.

3. Art and Culture

- Commission public murals, sculptures, and digital art that visualize wealth inequality as solvable—not fated.
- Encourage literature and cinema that depict **moral wealth**—not just material wealth—as aspirational.
- Frame stories around *"The first person who saved 10 million people anonymously."*

4. Faith and Philosophy

- Connect with interfaith organizations to frame the movement around *sacred obligation to care for the poor*.
- Create dialogues between theologians, monks, imams, rabbis, and priests around **economic justice as spiritual duty**.

FRAMING TRILLIONAIRES AS STEWARDS, **Not Villains**

This movement **does not depend on vilifying the wealthy.**

Instead, it reframes them as:

- **Entrusted, not entitled**
- **Chosen, not exempt**
- **Needed, not optional**

The goal is not shame—it's **irrefutable expectation.** By building a culture where stewardship is:

- Celebrated publicly,
- Verified openly,
- Required legally—

We create a new identity that **wealthy individuals will either embrace or reject with public consequence.**

CROWD TOOLS for **Public Pressure**

To keep momentum, we empower the public with **participatory tools:**

- **Contribution Trackers** – Displaying what percentage of obligation each trillionaire has fulfilled.
- **Red List Alerts** – Notifying when a steward fails to deliver, with options to organize, advocate, or publish open letters.
- **Green Badges** – Showing which contributors are exceeding expectations, linked to testimonials, data, and public response.

These tools **gamify participation** in planetary justice—without reducing it to metrics alone.

They make **accountability a shared act**, not a private protest.

What Success Looks Like

You'll know the message is working when:

- Trillionaires preemptively fulfill obligations to avoid public scrutiny.
- "Stewardship rating" becomes as important as credit score or market rank.
- Young people aspire not just to create billion-dollar companies—but to **lead with accountability** as a status symbol.
- Consumers demand that public-facing companies report **participation in the Humanity Guarantee Fund** alongside their profits.

13

TIMELINE TO GLOBAL IMPLEMENTATION – A DECADE TO CHANGE EVERYTHING

When the world begins to define greatness as generosity backed by structure.
Timeline to Global Implementation – A Decade to Change Everything
This isn't just a thought experiment.
It's a **ten-year blueprint.**
This section provides a **realistic, staged, and strategic implementation timeline** for building the full Trillionaire Responsibility Framework and Humanity Guarantee Fund —from the first public conversation to the final treaty enforcement.

If followed, this roadmap would mean that by **2035**, every trillionaire in the world is:

- **Legally enrolled** in a global survival stewardship system,
- **Publicly tracked** through open-access contribution ledgers,
- And **directly responsible** for the elimination of hunger and universal clean water access.

Let's break it down.

YEAR 1–2: **Cultural Ignition & Coalition Building**
Objectives:

- Launch book and story-based movement with multimedia global campaign.
- Build partnerships with journalists, educators, influencers, and thought leaders.
- Introduce concepts to multilateral organizations (UN, OECD, World Bank).
- Launch initial working group of ethics scholars, economists, technologists, and civil society leaders to draft the treaty framework.
- Begin prototyping **Digital Ledger of Stewardship** in beta form, tracking *voluntary* contributions.

Key Actions:

- Global op-eds: "It's Time to Make Trillionaires Responsible."
- Documentary shorts and animation explaining the Humanity Guarantee Fund.
- Formation of **The Founding Coalition for Stewardship** (20+ nations + civil society).

YEAR 3–4: **Pilot Programs and System Testing**
Objectives:

- Launch 3–5 regional humanitarian pilot programs fully funded and tracked through the voluntary beta Fund.
- Operationalize **live Digital Ledger** showing real-time results.
- Secure public endorsements from 2–3 prominent billionaires as **stewardship pioneers**.
- Begin drafting treaty and aligning legal architecture with existing international finance and tax treaties.

Key Actions:

- Youth-driven school projects in partnership with GCFWS beta platform.
- Global Citizen Jury prototype launched in select communities.
- Annual Stewardship Report published and distributed at major economic summits.

YEAR 5–6: Treaty Introduction and Early Signatures
Objectives:

- Introduce the **Global Treaty on Trillionaire Responsibility and Resource Contribution (GTTRRC)** at a UN Special Session.
- Secure initial 40+ nation signatures required to move forward via UN Charter Article 108.
- Begin global verification systems for net worth > $1T through third-party financial standards.

- Establish Tribunal for Stewardship Violations and Public Ethics Oversight Board.

Key Actions:

- Hold first **Global Stewardship Summit** showcasing success stories and political alignment.
- Begin public rating of contributors by fulfillment status.
- Launch global verification AI tools and whistleblower protections.

YEAR 7–8: Transition to Enforcement
Objectives:

- Ratify the treaty in 75+ countries, achieving enforceable international status.
- Automatically enroll first verified trillionaires under legal obligation to contribute annually.
- Execute first stewardship enforcement case via Tribunal.
- Expand Humanity Guarantee Fund to $100B/year minimum.

Key Actions:

- Announce real-time noncompliance indicators and triggers (red badges).
- Streamline contribution collection via smart

The Trillionaire Club

contracts, tax agencies, and digital financial systems.
• Educate public and media on legal rights to survival support.

YEAR 9–10: Global Norm Established
Objectives:

• Full integration of the Fund into UN systems and national aid distribution networks.
• Trillionaire stewardship becomes **mandatory, normalized, and transparent.**
• Fund achieves annual distribution capacity of $250–500B/year.
• Publish report: *"Ten Years to Universal Water and Food Security: The Trillionaire Era Begins."*

Key Actions:

• Host global education campaign: *"This System Is Yours."*
• Finalize citizen participation portals in every region.
• Expand fund oversight to include climate-related risk zones.

WHAT WE ACHIEVE **By Year 10**

- **Hunger ends** not as an aspiration, but as a statistical reality.
- **Water access** becomes a universal birthright.
- **Global power** becomes answerable— permanently and publicly.
- The first generation of trillionaire heirs is raised not in legacy of privilege, but **legacy of service.**
- The phrase *"too rich to care"* becomes an outdated joke.

And most importantly:
The global story shifts from *"Who will save us?"* to:
"We saved each other—with the tools we chose to build."
Bonus Chapter: America First in Stewardship – A New Kind of Global Leadership
Why the United States Must Lead the Trillionaire Responsibility Movement
There is a moment in every nation's history when it must choose between comfort and courage—between resting on its reputation and rising to the responsibility of a new age. For the United States, that moment is now.

This nation has long styled itself as the "leader of the free world." It has projected economic dominance, military power, technological supremacy, and cultural influence on a scale no civilization has matched in modern history. From the Marshall Plan to the moon landing, from Silicon Valley to the Internet, America has consistently claimed not just greatness—but **exceptionalism.**

But the 21st century asks for a new kind of leadership. Not dominance. Not disruption. But **moral governance over extreme power.**

Today, we live in a global landscape reshaped by wealth

The Trillionaire Club

accumulation that exceeds comprehension. Billionaires were once rare. Today, they are multiplying. And looming on the horizon is an inevitability the United States cannot ignore:

The first human being in history will soon possess a net worth of over one trillion dollars.

All credible projections suggest this person will likely be American—born or based in the U.S., building wealth through America's markets, data, labor, and law.

And that brings us to a question more important than their identity:

What will the United States do when one of its own holds more financial power than 90% of nations on Earth?

Will it watch and applaud?

Will it leave that power ungoverned?

Or will it step forward and **legislate a new form of civic duty**—one that finally matches the scale of 21st-century influence?

Why This Is Not a Radical Proposal—But a Necessary Evolution

The proposal laid out in this book—requiring any individual with a net worth of $1 trillion or more to join a globally coordinated stewardship framework to eliminate hunger and ensure access to clean water—is not an attack on capitalism. It is not a threat to innovation. It is not redistribution for redistribution's sake.

It is the next logical step in the evolution of ethical democracy.

It's what happens when:

- Markets succeed beyond their wildest dreams,

- Individuals accumulate public-impact power greater than sovereign states,
- And the public finally demands that **wealth serve life—not merely legacy.**

America already believes in proportional responsibility:

- Progressive taxation,
- Regulatory compliance,
- Corporate accountability.

We already mandate that wealth be transparent, fair, and governed.

What we have not done—yet—is extend those same principles to **extreme wealth on a historic scale.**

A trillion dollars is not a number.

It is a **public trust—whether the holder admits it or not.**

14

WHY THE U.S. MUST ACT FIRST

Why the U.S. Must Act First
If the United States passes a law—like the proposed *Trillionaire Stewardship Act*—requiring trillionaires to contribute proportionally to a globally governed food and water survival fund, it will:

- Become the first country to **ethically regulate ultra-high net worth citizens** in the interest of global humanity,
- Send a signal to allies, rivals, and undecided nations that **leadership still means something**,
- Restore **moral legitimacy** to the American project at a time when global trust in U.S. consistency has eroded,
- And redefine what "American exceptionalism" means in a world that no longer fears America's might—but questions its conscience.

This isn't about ideology.
It's about **existence**.

We are entering an age where climate collapse, global migration, resource wars, and digital monopolies will stress every system of cooperation and ethics we've built.

If America cannot govern its own most powerful citizens, what legitimacy does it have to ask others to follow suit?

THE HISTORICAL MOMENT **We're In**

The 20th century was shaped by ideological warfare—capitalism vs. communism, freedom vs. authoritarianism.

The 21st century is shaped by something subtler but more dangerous:

Scale without morality.

Technologies scale.

Fortunes scale.

But our sense of public duty hasn't kept up.

We've reached a point where an individual's wealth can:

- Reshape agricultural markets,
- Control supply chains,
- Withhold lifesaving water infrastructure from billions—by inaction alone.

The U.S. cannot legislate the entire world.

But it can do what it has always done when its conscience caught up with its courage:

- **Go first.**

AMERICA'S LEGACY **Hangs in the Balance**

Every generation of Americans has faced a defining moral challenge:

- The abolition of slavery,
- Women's suffrage,
- Civil rights,
- Marriage equality,
- Environmental protection.

Each time, we were told the change was "impossible," "unrealistic," "too radical."

Each time, someone led anyway.

And each time, the arc of American history bent closer to justice.

Now we face a challenge not of civil liberty alone, but of **global responsibility.**

Will we allow our richest citizens to rise without obligation?

Or will we enshrine in law the idea that **the highest accumulation demands the highest duty?**

Passing a national version of the Humanity Guarantee Framework is not just policy.

It's philosophy.

It's prophecy.

It's the next page in a Constitution that still imagines a government **of the people, by the people, and for the people**—all people, in all corners of the Earth.

Because survival is not national.

It is **human.**

Implementing the Framework Under U.S. Law – Practical Governance for a Moral Future

For a transformational idea to move from moral mandate to legislative muscle, it must be more than ethically sound. It must be **legally plausible, procedurally implementable, and constitutionally firm.** This part explores exactly how the **United States of America could turn the Humanity Guarantee Framework into national law**—not as a symbolic gesture, but as a fully enforceable and functional structure of accountability for its wealthiest citizens.

We begin not with theory, but with **legal realism**— grounded in American governance, economic precedent, and institutional readiness.

1. **Foundational Legal Authority: The Constitution and Congressional Power**

The U.S. Constitution provides **clear and robust pathways** for Congress to create and enforce a national stewardship requirement for ultra-high net worth individuals.

A. The Taxing and Spending Clause (Article I, Section 8, Clause 1)

This clause grants Congress the authority:

- To levy taxes,
- To collect duties,
- And to spend revenue "to provide for the common defense and general welfare of the United States."

A stewardship obligation framed as a **wealth-proportional humanitarian contribution** is entirely permissible under this clause, provided it advances the general welfare —defined in this context as eliminating global food and water insecurity, threats that directly affect U.S. stability, public health, migration pressure, and geopolitical risk.

B. The Commerce Clause (Article I, Section 8, Clause 3)

The Commerce Clause empowers Congress to regulate:

- Domestic and international trade,
- Financial transactions,
- Digital asset movement,
- And cross-border capital deployment.

Given that trillionaires typically operate through multi-jurisdictional financial ecosystems, the federal government has a compelling interest in:

- Regulating net worth concentration,
- Requiring accountability for asset deployment,
- And enforcing contribution standards tied to net financial impact.

C. Treaty Powers and Foreign Policy Authority

The Constitution gives the **President and Senate** authority to enter international treaties with foreign powers (Article II, Section 2). A law aligning the United States with a **Global Treaty on Trillionaire Responsibility** would be consistent with prior international humanitarian agreements (e.g., the Geneva Conventions, the Paris Climate Accord, the International Food Aid Convention).

2. Structuring the Stewardship Mandate: Key Components of Federal Legislation

The proposed law—tentatively titled the **Trillionaire Stewardship Act (TSA)**—would establish a statutory obligation for individuals with net worth exceeding $1 trillion to contribute annually to internationally governed food and water security infrastructure.

A. Threshold for Applicability

- Individuals must be verified as having a **net worth ≥ $1,000,000,000,000**, determined by a certified annual valuation audit.
- Net worth includes equity holdings, asset portfolios, cryptocurrencies, private business valuations, and global holdings.

B. Contribution Formula

- A progressive annual **stewardship levy** would be imposed:
    - 0.5% of net worth between $1T–$1.2T
    - 1.0% of net worth between $1.2T–$1.5T
    - 2.5% of all wealth above $1.5T
- Contributions are remitted to the **Office for Global Survival Obligations (OGSO)**—a new federal body under the Department of State or as a stand-alone stewardship commission.

C. Global Allocation

Funds would be disbursed through:

- U.S.-vetted international partners (e.g., USAID, World Food Programme, WHO),
- Treaty-aligned entities like the Global Committee for Food and Water Security (GCFWS),
- Third-party auditable humanitarian delivery networks.

No funds are held or administered unilaterally by foreign governments. All disbursements are subject to:

- Performance audits,
- GPS-verified delivery logs,
- And public impact tracking via the U.S. Stewardship Portal.

3. Enforcement and Penalties: When Wealth Fails to Serve

A law is only as powerful as its enforcement. The Trillionaire Stewardship Act would include robust accountability tools:

A. Verification Mechanism

- Annual net worth reporting required via IRS and SEC data integration.
- Failure to report or underreporting subject to felony misrepresentation penalties.

B. Delinquency Triggers

- Failure to contribute within 90 days of deadline results in:
  - Public listing on the Noncompliance Register,
  - Freezing of U.S.-based assets through Treasury and OFAC,
  - Denial of federal financial instruments (e.g., U.S. bond access, Fedwire clearance),

- Denial of government contracts or security-clearance–dependent ventures.

C. Persistent Noncompliance

- Multiple-year evasion results in civil forfeiture claims, international asset trace requests, and potential referral to the **International Tribunal for Stewardship Violations,** pending U.S. treaty ratification.

4. Administrative Infrastructure: The Office for Global Survival Obligations (OGSO)

The TSA would establish the OGSO as a federal commission with bipartisan governance and operational independence.

Core Responsibilities:

- Identify eligible individuals;
- Calculate contribution amounts;
- Collect, disburse, and audit funds;
- Coordinate with international partners;
- Maintain the **Digital Ledger of Stewardship**—a public, real-time contribution dashboard.

OGSO would also run:

- The **Citizen Oversight Council,** a rotating panel of public members,
- The **Stewardship Compliance Review Board,** staffed by ethics officers and forensic economists,

- A whistleblower protection and reward system for uncovering illegal avoidance schemes.

5. Legislative Strategy: How to Make It Pass in a Divided Congress

Though novel, this legislation is politically viable if framed correctly:

A. Appeal to American Values

- **Responsibility**: The wealthy built their fortunes with American infrastructure, IP law, education, and markets.
- **Patriotism**: Global hunger and water crises destabilize allies, drive migration, and breed extremism.
- **Leadership**: America can lead without war. This is soft power with real-world results.

B. Bipartisan Hooks

- For conservatives: fiscal discipline, global stability, private sector contribution.
- For progressives: equity, justice, moral alignment.
- For centrists: responsible capitalism and reputational sustainability.

C. Institutional Backing

- Think tank reports (Brookings, CFR, Cato),
- Endorsements from ethical billionaires (e.g., signatories of the Giving Pledge),

- Support from national security leaders emphasizing global risk mitigation.

6. Complementary Programs: Voluntary Billionaire Enrollment

The TSA could include a **voluntary "pre-trillionaire" pledge program:**

- Billionaires who enroll in stewardship responsibilities **before** hitting $1T receive:
    o Tax credits,
    o Public commendation,
    o Access to advisory roles within the OGSO network.

This aligns moral action with incentive—ensuring culture shifts alongside law.

PRACTICAL GOVERNANCE, **Moral Imperative**

The United States has all the legal power it needs to make this framework a reality.

What it requires now is **vision, courage,** and **the humility to govern excess** before excess governs us.

This is not just good law.

It's **the kind of law that restores belief in the republic.**

Because when the richest are held to account,

When the poorest are guaranteed survival,

And when governance becomes global—not through conquest, but through contribution—

Then, and only then, does America lead again.

15

DRAFT U.S. LEGISLATION – THE TRILLIONAIRE STEWARDSHIP ACT

Draft U.S. Legislation – The Trillionaire Stewardship Act

THE JOURNEY from moral idea to enforceable law must eventually take the form of a bill—shaped in language that can be debated, amended, passed, and enforced under U.S. legal authority. In this section, we present the **expanded, comprehensive draft** of the *Trillionaire Stewardship Act*, written in congressional legislative format, complete with definitions, enforcement mechanisms, administrative design, and global alignment language.

This version of the Act is designed to:

- Meet constitutional muster,
- Align with current tax and foreign aid mechanisms,
- Establish long-term bipartisan enforceability,

- And become a **model statute** that other nations could replicate or adopt through bilateral agreements.

TRILLIONAIRE STEWARDSHIP ACT of 2026
[TSA-2026]

SECTION 1. SHORT TITLE

This Act may be cited as the "**Trillionaire Stewardship Act of 2026.**"

SECTION 2. FINDINGS AND PURPOSE

(a) **Congressional Findings:**

1. In the 21st century, private individuals may possess wealth exceeding the GDP of entire nations, necessitating new models of civic responsibility.
2. Extreme wealth creates structural influence and global impact beyond the scope of voluntary philanthropy or domestic taxation alone.
3. Hunger and lack of access to clean water remain two of the most solvable human crises, requiring sustainable funding mechanisms commensurate with modern private wealth capacity.
4. American innovation, infrastructure, and markets enable the creation of such wealth; therefore, its highest tiers must contribute

proportionally to preserving global life, stability, and dignity.

(b) Purpose:
The purpose of this Act is to:

- Legally require U.S.-based trillionaires to contribute annually to internationally governed food and water security efforts;
- Establish a transparent, auditable mechanism for stewardship accountability;
- Reaffirm the United States' global leadership in humanitarian innovation and responsible capitalism.

SECTION 3. DEFINITIONS
As used in this Act:

1. **Trillionaire** – A natural person, citizen or legal resident of the United States, whose global net worth equals or exceeds $1,000,000,000,000 USD, as certified annually by the Office of Global Survival Obligations (OGSO).
2. **Net Worth** – Total verified assets, including publicly and privately held stocks, equity in closely held corporations, real estate, digital assets, offshore holdings, trusts, cash reserves, and intellectual property valuation.
3. **Stewardship Contribution** – The annual percentage of a trillionaire's net worth, as defined

by this Act, required to be remitted to the Humanity Guarantee Fund via OGSO.
4. **OGSO** – A federally chartered independent commission tasked with enforcement and oversight of all stewardship-related obligations.
5. **Noncompliance** – Failure to remit required contributions, refusal to verify net worth, or the obstruction of any aspect of OGSO review or international coordination.

SECTION 4. STEWARDSHIP OBLIGATION THRESHOLDS AND FORMULA

(a) **Contribution Schedule:**

Trillionaire individuals are required to remit annually the following:

- 0.5% of net worth between $1 trillion and $1.2 trillion
- 1.0% of net worth between $1.2 trillion and $1.5 trillion
- 2.5% of any net worth in excess of $1.5 trillion

(b) **Contribution Floor and Ceiling:**

- The minimum annual contribution may not be less than $5 billion USD.
- The total contribution may not exceed 2.5% of verified net worth without voluntary election or Tribunal penalty.

(c) **Indexing for Inflation:**

The Trillionaire Club

The contribution thresholds will be recalibrated every 5 years by the Secretary of the Treasury, in alignment with the Consumer Price Index (CPI) and global income distribution standards.

SECTION 5. ESTABLISHMENT OF THE OFFICE FOR GLOBAL SURVIVAL OBLIGATIONS (OGSO)

(a) **Structure and Authority:**

- OGSO shall be established as an independent federal agency with administrative, enforcement, and audit powers.
- OGSO shall be led by a nonpartisan **Stewardship Commission**, composed of five presidential appointees with staggered ten-year terms, confirmed by the Senate.

(b) **Duties:**

- Certify and verify net worth of qualifying individuals annually.
- Calculate and collect annual contributions.
- Collaborate with the Department of State, USAID, and treaty-aligned international organizations for disbursement.
- Maintain and publish a real-time **Digital Ledger of Stewardship**.
- Investigate suspected avoidance, delay, fraud, or interference.

(c) **Reporting Requirements:**

- OGSO must report annually to Congress on:
  - Funds collected,
  - Impact metrics,
  - Compliance status,
  - Citizen oversight data,
  - Any enforcement proceedings.

SECTION 6. ENFORCEMENT AND PENALTIES

(a) Failure to Report:

- Up to $100 million in fines,
- Compelled financial disclosure through the Department of the Treasury.

(b) Failure to Contribute (Delinquency >180 days):

- Public listing on **Stewardship Delinquency Register**,
- Freezing of all U.S.-based digital and physical financial accounts,
- Denial of federal licenses, procurement contracts, and market privileges.

(c) **Evasion, Fraud, or Willful Misreporting:**

- Civil fines up to three times the unpaid contribution,
- Referral to the U.S. Department of Justice for criminal investigation,
- Ineligibility for participation in sovereign

investment, defense contracting, or privileged partnerships.

SECTION 7. GLOBAL COORDINATION AND TREATY ALIGNMENT

(a) **International Cooperation:**

The Secretary of State, in consultation with OGSO and relevant agencies, shall initiate formal alignment of this Act with:

- The United Nations Global Committee for Food and Water Security (GCFWS),
- The World Bank

16

DRAFT UNITED NATIONS GENERAL ASSEMBLY RESOLUTION

Draft United Nations General Assembly Resolution
Resolution Title:
Toward the Elimination of Global Hunger and Universal Access to Clean Water through Proportional Responsibility of Ultra-High-Net-Worth Individuals
Sponsors: [To be filled by sponsoring nations]
Co-sponsors: [To be determined]

THE GENERAL ASSEMBLY,
Guided by the purposes and principles of the Charter of the United Nations, particularly the promotion of social progress, dignity, and better standards of life in larger freedom,
Reaffirming that the right to adequate food and the right to safe and clean drinking water are fundamental human rights essential for the full enjoyment of life and all other rights, as recognized in General Assembly resolutions

64/292 and 70/169, and codified in international human rights treaties,

Deeply concerned that more than 800 million people continue to suffer from chronic hunger and over 2 billion lack access to safe drinking water, despite existing global resources, technologies, and financial capabilities,

Recognizing the emergence of unprecedented personal wealth in the modern era, including individuals whose net worth surpasses one trillion United States dollars,

Affirming that with such extraordinary wealth must come extraordinary responsibility to serve humanity and alleviate preventable suffering,

Determined to establish effective, transparent, and enforceable systems of global cooperation to eliminate hunger and ensure universal access to clean water by the year 2035,

1. Declares that the elimination of hunger and provision of universal access to clean, safe drinking water shall be considered global moral and developmental imperatives for the 21st century;

2. Proposes the creation of a Global Committee for Food and Water Security (GCFWS) composed of all individuals whose personal net worth exceeds one trillion United States dollars, tasked with:

a. Collaborating with the United Nations and relevant international agencies (e.g., FAO, WFP, WHO, UNICEF) to assess annual global food and water needs,

b. Providing proportional financial contributions based on global need forecasts and committee membership size,

c. Funding infrastructure, logistics, and programmatic interventions to eliminate hunger and ensure water access,

d. Ensuring full transparency through a publicly accessible accountability dashboard and independent annual audit;

3. Emphasizes that participation in the Committee shall be automatic and binding upon reaching the trillion-dollar wealth threshold, and that failure to meet agreed targets for global food and water security shall trigger a proportional responsibility surcharge, equitably distributed among Committee members to fully fund any remaining unmet needs;

4. Requests the Secretary-General to convene a high-level panel of experts to produce a comprehensive implementation framework within 12 months, in consultation with Member States, civil society, and global development partners;

5. Encourages Member States to explore legislative and treaty-based pathways to codify financial responsibility mechanisms for ultra-high-net-worth individuals in the interest of eliminating hunger and water insecurity;

6. Calls upon public and private stakeholders to champion this initiative and integrate it into Sustainable Development Goals 2 (Zero Hunger) and 6 (Clean Water and Sanitation) financing strategies;

7. Recommends the adoption of global indicators to track progress on eliminating hunger and water scarcity that are linked directly to contributions from ultra-wealthy individuals and their philanthropic or logistical initiatives;

8. Decides to include this resolution as a permanent agenda item under "Sustainable Development: Implementation of the 2030 Agenda" and to remain actively seized of the matter.

EPILOGUE – WHAT COMES AFTER ENOUGH

At some point, you stop counting.
Not because the numbers cease to grow,
But because **you've finally built something bigger than yourself.**

This book began with a simple question:

What would it mean if the richest people on Earth were legally required to end hunger and ensure clean water—for everyone?

The answer was not a donation.

It was not an app.

It was not a campaign.

The answer was a **global structure of responsibility:**

- Built on enforcement, not goodwill.
- Governed by transparency, not sentiment.
- Powered by a belief that **there is such a thing as "enough."**

When Enough Becomes a Threshold

A trillion dollars is not wealth.
It is **a pressure system**.
It bends markets.
Moves politics.
Alters ecosystems.
And for too long, it's gone **unchecked**.
But once the world decides:

- That enough is not just an amount—it's a **mandate**,
- That extreme wealth is not private property—but **global custodianship**,
- That survival is not optional—but **a guaranteed right**—

Then we cross a threshold.
From scarcity to structure.
From asking to requiring.
From charity to **justice codified**.

What Happens After the First Trillionaire Pays Their Due?

Everything changes.

- Not just for the child who gets a hot meal or the village that drinks clean water.
- But for the trillionaire themselves—who is finally seen **not as an anomaly**, but as a participant in human solidarity.

They stop building rocket ships.

They start building **root systems**.
They stop talking about legacy.
And start living it—**one fulfilled obligation at a time**.
And when others see them, they don't see a tycoon.
They see **a steward**.

THE FINAL TURNING **Point**
This is not just a book.
It is an invitation.
To:

- The public—who now knows what to demand.
- The policymakers—who now know how to enforce it.
- The next generation—who now sees that wealth can mean more than exclusion.

And to the first trillionaire reading this, or the one who will soon arrive:
You will not be asked.
You will be expected.
Not because we hate your wealth—
But because **we finally understand what it's for.**
To feed.
To heal.
To serve.
Not someday.
Not if you feel like it.
Now.

THE WORLD **After Enough**

And what comes after?
A world where:

- Greatness is measured in **how many lives you lifted.**
- Wealth is not your wall—but your bridge.
- And being the richest person on Earth means one thing only:

You are **responsible for everyone else's survival.**
And that, finally,
Is **enough.**

AFTERWORD

Dear Future Trillionaire,
You may not know me.
But I know something about you.
I know that by the time you read this, you will have reached a threshold no human in history has ever crossed:
A trillion dollars in personal wealth.
You will have created, accumulated, or stewarded more capital than entire nations.
You will sit atop systems of finance, labor, infrastructure, and innovation that have reshaped the planet.
And you will be celebrated for your vision, your leadership, your success.
But there is one question that success cannot answer:
Now that you have more than enough—what will you do with it?
Not *how will you spend it.*
Not *how will you protect it.*
Not *how will you grow it further.*
What will you do for the world that made it possible?

Because whether you realize it or not, you did not build your empire alone.

You stand on the labor of billions.

On roads and code and data you did not lay.

On clean air and safe water and legal systems and educators and first responders and anonymous hands you will never meet.

You did not succeed in isolation.

So you must not remain powerful in isolation.

There is a framework waiting for you.

It is called the **Humanity Guarantee Fund**.

It is a structure—not a charity. A covenant—not a campaign.

A global mechanism that transforms excess wealth into the most necessary infrastructure on Earth:

- Universal access to food.
- Universal access to clean water.
- Universal enforcement of survival as a right—not a favor.

If the world has not yet adopted this framework by the time you read this, let this letter be the first proposal placed at your feet.

Not as a plea.

As a promise:

There is a better way to be the richest person alive.

You have the opportunity to **go first**,

To volunteer what will one day be legally required,

To lead by obligation before it is mandated by law.

You can make history not just for what you built—

But for what you gave back.

For what you made **possible** for those who will never know your name, but will survive because you acted.

And if this framework *has* already been adopted, then this letter is a different kind of invitation:
Join it not grudgingly, but **wholeheartedly.**
Join it not because you must—but because you **choose to define wealth as service, not separation.**
Let your name be the first in green on the Digital Ledger of Stewardship.
Let your leadership be measured in lives sustained, not just deals struck.
Let your greatness be *how many others get to live full lives* because you stopped asking "What more can I own?" and started asking "What more can I fix?"

The world does not need another monument to ego.
It needs an architect of equity.
And now, with your wealth, your voice, and your decision, you can be that.
Go first.
Give boldly.
Lead responsibly.
And let history remember you not for your trillion,
But for what you chose to do with it.
Sincerely,
JD Rossetti
One of Eight Billion
On behalf of a world ready to survive—if only you help us build the structure to do so.

ABOUT THE AUTHOR

JD Rossetti is a seasoned public affairs professional, which is a fancy way of saying he's spent over a decade navigating the world of government relations, legislative affairs, public administration, and policy analysis—without losing his sense of humor (or his hair... mostly). With a knack for advocacy, strategic planning, and community engagement, JD has dedicated his career to shaping public policy and making a real difference.

A former Washington State Representative, JD tackled big issues like education, infrastructure, economic development, and public health—because someone had to. He successfully secured funding for education, mental health initiatives, and broadband expansion, ensuring that students could learn, communities could thrive, and people could finally stream their favorite shows without buffering. As a School Board Director, he championed student success, technology integration, and budget oversight, proving that yes, numbers can be fun (sometimes).

JD holds a Master of Public Administration (MPA) from The Evergreen State College and a Bachelor of Arts in Public Affairs from Washington State University. Passionate about public service, policy innovation, and effective governance, JD continues to work toward policies that strengthen and support communities—one well-crafted policy (and dad joke) at a time.

www.ingramcontent.com/pod-product-compliance
Lightning Source LLC
Chambersburg PA
CBHW020535030426
42337CB00013B/859